Insight
THE SPIRITUAL REALM

UNDERSTANDING WHAT TRANSPIRES
IN THE REALM OF THE SPIRIT

VICTOR O. SODIMU

Insight Into THE SPIRITUAL REALM

Copyright © 2009 by Victor O. Sodimu.
All rights reserved
Unless otherwise indicated, all scripture quotations are taken from the *New International Version* translation of the Bible.

Other scripture quotations are taken from the *King James Version (KJV)*, *New American Standard Bible (NASB)* and *New Living Translation (NLT)*.

All enquiries and trade orders to:
Victor O. Sodimu
14 Russel View
Russel Square
Fortunestown
Dublin 24, Ireland 353
E-mail: **victorsodimu@yahoo.com**

Printed by: supreme**printers**.com

No part of this book may be reproduced or transmitted in any form or by any means, electronic or mechanical – including photocopying, recording, or by any information storage and retrieval system – without permission in writing from the author.

ISBN: 978-0-9563431-0-9

TABLE OF CONTENTS

	DEDICATION	4
	ACKNOWLEDGMENTS	5
	PREFACE	7
1.	GOD THE ETERNAL SPIRIT AND KING	9
2.	SATANIC SPIRITUAL KINGDOM	21
3.	THE SPIRITUAL BEGAT THE PHYSICAL	27
4.	MOVEMENTS IN THE SPIRITUAL REALM	39
5.	THIS COMPLICATED WORLD	55
6.	WHAT HAPPENS WHEN A MAN DIES?	59
7.	THE SPIRIT-MAN'S EXPERIENCE OUTSIDE THE BODY	71
8.	SATANIC INFLUENCES OVER THIS PRESENT WORLD	83
9.	SPECIFIC SATANIC MANIPULATIONS	91
10.	THE HEIRS OF GOD'S KINGDOM	115
11.	CALLED TO DOUBLE UNDERSTANDING	129
12.	DON'T ALLOW SATAN AND HIS AGENTS OPPRESS YOU	139
13.	PRAYERS AND CONFESSIONS	153

DEDICATION

I dedicate this great book to my glorious Teacher and Counsellor, the Holy Spirit, who taught me and opened my spiritual understanding into the things of God (1 CORINTHIANS 2: 12).

Also to my wonderful wife, who supported me throughout the writing of this project. All glory be to God.

ACKNOWLEDGEMENT

With special thanks:

To Elder Adegboyega Oyelade who took time to proof-read and edit this book. I appreciate your counsel and suggestions that have contributed immensely to the success of this project. My God will continuously lift your family up in Jesus name.

To my wonderful sister in Christ, who typed some portions of this book, Damilola Oduwole. Wherever this book circulates to, your name and contribution will be mentioned. God will shield your life with favour.

To my Irish Christian sister, Carmel Whelan, who was one of the people that made me see the necessity to write this book. God will reward you greatly.

To Pastor and Mrs Olufemi-Ojo, I call you "my helper of destiny" because the Lord greatly used you for me to fulfil His divine purpose for my life. No man except God can reward you both and He will do so beyond human imagination. And also to Pastor Peter Amujo, for your spiritual advice towards the success of this book. You are wonderful sir, my God will bless your ministry.

To my fathers in the Lord who have contributed to my spiritual growth: Pastor Olu Omotara, Reverend Andrew Oyinlola, Pastor A.O. Fasina and many others that I could not mention. I appreciate you all for your fatherly counsels.

To my mentors whose books and ministries have helped me immensely: Pastor E.H.L. Olusheye president CAC worldwide, Brother Gbile Akanni of Living Seed Ministries, Dr. D.K. Olukoya the General Overseer of MFM Worldwide, Pastor W.F. Kumuyi the General Overseer of Deeper Life Bible Church, Pastor E.A. Adeboye the General Overseer of RCCG Worldwide, Pastor David Oyedepo the General Overseer of Living Faith Ministries Worldwide, Reverend Kenneth E. Hagin and Watchman Nee (of blessed memories). And to many others all over the world, which I cannot mention now. God will keep you to the end in Jesus name.

Finally to my loving wife Olubunmi, for her unflinching moral and spiritual support, especially for sustaining the home front while I am busy in the field. God bless you.

PREFACE |

Many Children of our God Almighty are so afraid of those who are afraid of them, and they run away from those who should be running away from them. Why? Any true born again child of God is stronger, wiser, and mightier than the devil the father of all evil people and liars. And you know what; your enemies know that if you know your position with Christ in God, they have no dominion over you. The degree of ferocious satanic activities towards any child of God shows the extent to which they are scared of you.

You are the child of a loving God, the child of destiny. No weapon fashion against you shall prosper if you know your Father, God Almighty and your position in His kingdom. No affliction, suffering, persecution and evil work can kill you. You are stronger, mightier and above them all because you life is in the hand of God.

Have you been running around fearing Satan and his wicked angels? My God wants you to stop running now; He wants you to put Satan where he belongs under you feet. Stand in your position that God has put you in Christ. It is time to put Satan down and raise God higher.

This book *"Insight Into The Spiritual Realm"* will open your inner eyes and mind to know the trick of

Satan and his limited power against the power of our Lord and Saviour Jesus Christ, which is not limited. In the name of Jesus every knee shall bow. There is no negotiation; the Word of God is final. Call Satan's bluff today and stand in the blood of Jesus Christ. The fact is that whatever happens in the spiritual realm will always affect us whether we believe it or not.

The knowledge you gain from this book together with your Bible will open your inner eyes and mind more to live for God and to harass the satanic kingdom with the blood of Christ and the testimony of Christ.

I totally recommend this book, as it will make you to apply the principle of Gods Word to take you to higher heights. Happy reading.

PASTOR A.O. FASHINA
CHAIRMAN CHRIST APOSTOLIC CHURCH OUTREACH DISTRICT HQ

CHAPTER ONE

GOD THE ETERNAL SPIRIT AND KING |

The Lord Jesus Christ clearly stated in **JOHN 4:24** that *"God is Spirit..."* Apostle Paul further revealed some information to us about this same God:

1 TIMOTHY 1: 17
"Now unto the king eternal, immortal, invisible, the only wise God, be honour and glory for ever and ever. Amen."

Four important qualities are revealed about God in the above scripture: He is eternal, connoting that He has always existed and will forever exist. He has no beginning and ending. He is from eternity to eternity.

He is immortal, depicting that He is not mortal doomed for death, but divine. He is unfading, incorruptible and, He lives forevermore.

His invisible quality means that He cannot be seen with mere mortal eyes, not even with the aid of technological equipment, because He is a spirit being.

This Spirit-God is "the only wise God": He is the source of all wisdom. By wisdom He created the whole universe. He gives wisdom to the wise, and about His wisdom, the Bible says, no one can fathom. Apostle Paul thought deeply about this mysterious God and finally exclaimed:

ROMANS 11: 33-36 NASB
"Oh, the dept of the riches both of the wisdom and knowledge of God! How unsearchable are His judgements and unfathomable His ways! For who has known the mind of the Lord, or who became His counsellor? Or who has first given to Him that it might be paid back to Him again? For from Him and through Him and to Him are all things. To Him is the glory forever. Amen."

EXISTENCE OF LIFE

Life had been in the spiritual realm for uncountable years before it ever existed in the physical realm here on earth. God the Eternal Spirit and King had created all things for Himself in the spiritual planet called heaven before the planet earth ever existed. Heavenly hosts i.e. the cherubim and seraphim, the powerful angels, and all other heavenly creatures were, and are serving and attending unto this Great Spirit-God. To Him be the glory forever! Heaven has been well established and organised from eternity. This is beyond human comprehension.

In the book of Isaiah and Revelation we see how God enabled His chosen Prophet and Apostle to see into the spiritual realm of heaven. One can only see into the spiritual realm through what is called *"the spiritual eyes"*, and because a part of the natural man is also made of the spirit, God sometimes permits man to catch the glimpse of the spiritual realm. (More of this will be dealt with in preceding chapter).

When his spiritual eyes were opened, Prophet Isaiah cried out:

ISAIAH 6: 1-4

"...I saw the Lord seated on a throne, high and exalted, and the train of His robe filled the temple. Above him were seraphs, each with six wings: With two wings they covered their faces, with two they covered their feet, and with two they were flying. And they were calling to one another: "Holy, holy, holy is the LORD Almighty; the whole earth is full of his glory." At the sound of their voices the doorposts and thresholds shook and the temple was filled with smoke."

Let us read also the vision of Apostle John on the Island of Patmos:

REVELATION 4: 1-11; 5:11-14 NLT
"...Then as I looked, I saw a door standing open in heaven, and the same voice I heard before spoke to me with the sound of a mighty trumpet blast. The voice said, "come up here, and I will show you what must happen after these things." And instantly I WAS IN THE SPIRIT and I saw a throne in heaven and some one sitting on it! The one sitting on it was as brilliant as gemstones-jasper and carnelian. And the glow of an emerald circled his throne like a rainbow. Twenty-four thrones surrounded him, and twenty-four elders sat on them. They were all clothed in white and had gold crowns on their heads. And from the throne came flashes of lightning and the rumble of thunder. And in front of the throne were seven lamp-stands with burning flames. They are the seven spirits of God. In front of the throne was a shiny sea of glass, sparkling like crystal. In the center and around the throne were four living beings, each covered with eyes, front and back. The first of these living beings had the form of a lion; the second looked like an ox; the third had a human face; and the fourth had the form of an eagle with wings spread out as though in flight. Each of these living beings had six wings, and their wings were covered with eyes, inside and out. Day after day and night after night they keep on saying,

"Holy, holy, holy is the lord God Almighty- the

one who always was, who is, and who is still to come." Whenever the living beings give glory and honor and thanks to the one sitting on the throne, the one who live forever and ever, the twenty-four elders fall down and worship the one who lives forever and ever. And they lay their crowns before the throne and say, "You are worthy, O Lord our God, to receive glory and honor and power. For you created everything, and it is for your pleasure that they exist and were created.".... Then I looked again, and I heard the singing of thousands and millions of angels around the throne and the living beings and the elders. And they sang in a mighty chorus: "The lamb is worthy- the lamb who was killed. He is worthy to receive power and riches and wisdom and strength and honor and glory and blessing." And then I heard every creature in heaven and on earth and under the earth and in the sea. They also sang: "Blessing and honor and glory and power belong to the one sitting on the throne and to the lamb forever and ever." And the four living beings said, "amen!" And the twenty-four elders fell down and worshiped God and the Lamb."

One of the things we notice from **REVELATION 4** above is that the appearance of God is too awesome to be seen even in the realm of the spirit. John could see the cherubim, the angels, the elders, the thrones, and the sea of glass but could not see God. He only beheld His glorious appearance.

Although God is likewise a spirit, He is more glorious and more invisible even in the realm of the spirit. He is the glorious Eternal Spirit that created all other spirit beings. Halleluah!

When Job began to question God's judgement because of the problem he was passing through, God responded with series of questions to let him realize that he didn't have the wisdom to question Him:

JOB 38: 4-7
"Where were you when I laid the earth's foundation? Tell me, if you understand. Who marked off its dimensions? Surely you know! Who stretched a measuring line across it? On what were its footings set, or who laid its cornerstone – WHILE THE MORNING STARS SANG TOGETHER AND ALL THE ANGELS SHOUTED FOR JOY?"

All angels were shouting and singing for joy when God was creating the world. No one could fathom how long ago the heaven had existed before God decided to create human beings and the entire physical world. The spirit beings existed far before the human beings. They are the hosts of heaven and are all witnesses to the beginning of lives on planet earth. We all must understand this truth.

SPIRIT BEINGS & HUMAN BEINGS

There are mainly two realms of lives in existence; these are the spiritual and physical realms. Human beings, animals, trees and others alike in this earth dwell in the physical realm while the spirit beings occupy the spiritual realm. Life does not originate from the physical but from the spiritual. Lives have been in the spiritual realm for probably several billions of years before it ever existed in the physical realm.

But who are these spirit beings? How can we really understand their existence? One way to approach these questions is to first study the nature of human beings as this pertains to us. We understand from the word of God that the human being is made up of three parts: the spirit, the soul and the body.

> 1 THESSALONIANS 5: 23 KJV
> "And the very God of peace sanctify you wholly; and I pray GOD YOUR WHOLE SPIRIT AND SOUL AND BODY be preserved blameless unto the coming of our Lord Jesus Christ"

The whole or complete man as confirmed in the scripture above is the spirit, the soul and the body. The spirit part of the human being is the same as that of the spirit beings (we shall talk explicitly on this in the preceding chapter). The soul of man comprises the will, the mind and the emotion. In our mind we think, imagine, and judge. Through our emotion we express love, happiness, joy, sorrow, sadness etc. All determination, willingness and unwillingness to do things are functions of man's will. All these are in the compartment of man called the soul. The body of man is the physical part of man that associates with the physical world. As human beings we all recognise ourselves by our physical appearance.

Furthermore, the word of God tells us that things in the physical realm are shadows or images of those in the spiritual realm. We have numerous examples in the scripture to confirm this, let us consider of them:

In **GENESIS 1:26**, during the creation *"God said, Let us make man in our own image, after our likeness..."* In the wilderness God warned Moses to build the tabernacle according to the pattern of the temple in heaven.

HEBREWS 8: 5 NLT
"THEY SERVE IN A PLACE OF WORSHIP THAT IS ONLY A COPY, A SHADOW OF REAL ONE IN HEAVEN. For when Moses was getting ready to build the tabernacle, God gave him this warning: "Be sure that you make everything according to the design I have shown you here on the mountain".

We confirmed both in Isaiah 6:1-4 and Revelation 4:1-11 earlier that there had been a temple in heaven. According to the book of Hebrew this is the real and perfect temple that our Lord Jesus Christ entered with His blood as our Eternal High Priest and presently intercedes for us.

Hebrews 8: 1, 2
"The point of what we are is this: we do have such a high priest, who sat down at the right hand of the throne of the Majesty in heaven, and WHO SERVES IN THE SANCTUARY, THE TRUE TABERNACLE SET UP BY THE LORD, NOT BY MAN."

This shows that physical beings are designed in the similarity of the spirit beings. These spirit beings are mainly angels created by God who Himself is also an Eternal Spirit as we have studied earlier. The spirit beings also have their soul: they think and imagine; they express love, happiness, joy, sadness, anger etc, just like human beings. Numerous examples of this abound in the scriptures:

After the Lord God had driven Adam and Eve out of the Garden of Eden, He placed a powerful Cherub with a flaming sword to keep the way of the tree of life (Genesis 3: 24).

God had to warn the Israelites not to be rebellious against the angel He sent to guide them otherwise he (the angel) would be angry and would not forgive them (EXODUS 23: 20-23). No doubt, they are stronger and more intelligent than us.

Likewise they have a body like we human's and it functions like ours'; they have eyes, mouth, legs etc.; they are more real than we are in this physical world. Various scriptural verses show us that angels have the parts of the body, which we as human beings have, let us consider the scripture below:

REVELATION 10: 1-3
"Then I saw another mighty angel coming down from heaven. He was robed in a cloud, with a rainbow above HIS HEAD; HIS FACE was like the sun, and HIS LEGS were like fiery pillars. He was holding a little scroll, which lay open in HIS HANDS. He planted his RIGHT FOOT on the sea and his LEFT FOOT on the land, and HE GAVE A LOUD SHOUT like the roar of a lion..."

Someone may ask, *"Do angels eat?"* Well the answer is found in the book of PSALM 78: 25, *"Men ate the bread of angels..."*

Another may also ask, are you saying human beings are created in the image of the angels? Human beings may not exactly be like the angels but many of the qualities in them are also in us. Moreover Jesus Christ, speaking of those who will partake in the first resurrection, says *"and they can no longer die; FOR THEY ARE LIKE THE*

ANGELS..." (LUKE 20:36). God who is the Eternal Spirit created the angels as spirit beings like Himself, and also created human beings in His own image. Both men and angels are His creatures; definitely we both share some things in common with our creator.

There are some differences however, between spirit beings and human beings. The Lord Jesus tells us they do not reproduce, and they do not marry as we do here on earth.

LUKE 20:34-36
"Jesus replied, 'the people of this age marry and are given in marriage. But those who are considered worthy of taking part in that age and in the resurrection from the dead will neither marry nor be given in marriage, and they can no longer die; for they are like the angels. They are God's children, since they are children of the resurrection'."

The Lord also says that the spirit beings don't die as human beings die here on earth. Their body is also different from ours in that they have what is called *"the celestial or spiritual body"*.

1 CORINTHIANS 15:40, 44. KJV
"There are also celestial bodies and bodies terrestrial: but the glory of the celestial is one, and the glory of the terrestrial is another ...there is a natural body, and there is a spiritual body."

God moulds our own body from the soil and it is heading for death.

Genesis 2:7; 3:19 KJV
"And the Lord God formed man out of the dust of the ground, and breathed into his nostrils the breath of life; and man became a living soul...In the sweat of thy face shalt thou eat bread, till thou return unto the ground; for out of it wast thou taken: for dust thou art, and unto dust shalt thou return."

This implies that our individual lives in the body on earth have an expiry date; the day it expires then we die. But spirit beings will never die; they are created to exist eternally.

They are not limited by physical barriers like human beings; they can move through the walls, move in the wind and are considerably faster than us in all things.

Although the same God created the spirit beings and human beings, the former are of higher life than the human beings, they have been in existence before us, and are more intelligent and powerful.

Psalms 8:4, 5
"What is man that you are mindful of him, the son of man that you care for him? You made him a little lower than the heavenly beings and crown him with glory and honor."

CHAPTER TWO

SATANIC SPIRITUAL KINGDOM |

We must understand that in the realm of the spirit there are mainly two kingdoms namely: the kingdom of God and the kingdom of Satan. In the earlier chapter we discussed the spiritual kingdom of God, which is the only true eternal kingdom.

However, before the physical world ever existed, another rebellious kingdom pulled off from the kingdom of God through a rebellious archangel called Lucifer who became Satan the devil because of his rebellion against God his creator. The word *"Satan"* means the adversary. He opposed the authority of God in heaven and further plotted a coup to overthrow his creator. He is the first coup plotter and the father of all coups plotters.

ISAIAH. 14: 12-15 KJV.
"How art thou fallen from heaven, O Lucifer, son of the morning! How art thou cut down to the ground, which didst weaken the nation! For thou hast said in thine heart, I will ascend into

heaven, I will exalt my throne above the stars of God: I will sit also upon the mount of the congregation, in the sides of the north, I will ascend above the heights of the clouds; I will be like the most High. Yet, thou shall be brought down to hell, to the sides of the pit."

He fell because of pride and God banished him and his rebellious angels from the highest heaven.

In the Old Testament part of the scripture we read that although Satan and his evil angels were cast out of heaven, he still had the guts to go there to present himself before God among the angels. He also walked to and fro the earth and was able to accuse a righteous man, Job, before God. Bible calls him the accuser of the brethren (**REVELATIONS 12: 10**).

JOB 1:6-11 NLT

"One day the angels came to present themselves before the LORD, and Satan the Accuser came with them. "Where have you come from?" the LORD asked Satan. And Satan answered the LORD; "I have been going back and forth across the earth, watching everything that's going on." Then the LORD asked Satan, "Have you noticed my servant Job? He is the finest man in all the earth – a man of complete integrity. He fears God and will have nothing to do with evil." Satan replied to the LORD, "Yes, Job fears God, but not without good reason! You have always protected him and his home and his property from harm. You made him prosperous in every thing he does. Look how rich he is! But take away everything he has, and he will surely curse you to your face!"

But in the New Testament we see another great light about Satan and his rebellious spirit beings:

REVELATION 12: 7-9
"And there was war in heaven. Michael and his angels fought against the dragon, and the dragon and his angels fought back. But he was not strong enough, and they lost their place in heaven. The great dragon was hurled down-that ancient serpent called the devil, or Satan, who leads the whole world astray. He was hurled to the earth, and his angels with him."

In **Verse 11** of the same chapter above, the Bible says the angels of God in heaven overcame the devil by the ***BLOOD OF THE LAMB*** *and the words of their testimony*. This means that it is the blood of Jesus; and the testimony of His death, resurrection and ascension to the throne in heaven, that conquers Satan. The angels used this truth against Satan and his hosts in battle, although he fought against the truth, yet he could not prevail and was hurled out of heaven. The word of God says, *"For we can do nothing against the truth, but for the truth."* (2 CORINTHIANS 13: 8 KJV).

Now there is no more a place for the devil in the highest heaven. He has been finally cast out with no chance of returning there again unlike what we saw earlier in the case of Job. Some Christians still believe that Satan can still go to heaven to accuse them. No, it is no more possible! Why? The Lord Jesus Christ who defeated the devil is now seated enthroned in heaven. Christ Jesus cannot share the heaven with the devil!

EPHESIANS 1: 19-21 KJV.

"...the working of his (God) mighty power, which he wrought in Christ, when he raised him from the dead, and set him at his own right hand in the heavenly places, far above all principalities, and power, and might, and dominion, and every name that is named, not only in this world, but also in that which is to come."

There is a wide gap now between Christ Jesus and Satan in the heavenly realm.

Does it mean that Satan can't accuse us again? Of course he still does but not in heaven but here on earth. The children of God need not be afraid of him or his demons, we are told in **JAMES 4:7** to resist the devil, and he will flee from us in Jesus name.

SATAN'S DOMAIN

We can take inference from various other scriptures that Satan and his evil spirits have pitched their kingdom in three regions in the universe:

HEAVENLY REALM

This is not the heaven where God rules. God's word tells us that there are levels in the heavenly. While Solomon was dedicating the temple he prayed:

> **1 KINGS 8:27**
> "But will God really dwell on earth? The heavens, even the highest heaven, cannot contain you..."

Apostle Paul confirms that there are three heavens.

> **2 CORINTHIANS 12: 2**
> "I know a man in Christ who fourteen years ago was caught up to the third heaven. Whether it was in the body or out of the body I do not know - God knows."

He also tells us that satanic kingdom is in the heavenlies waging spiritual warfare against the saints:

> **EPHESIANS 6:12 NASB**
> "For our struggle is not against flesh and blood, but against the rulers, against the powers, against the world forces of this darkness, against the spiritual forces of wickedness in the heavenly places."

We therefore conclude that God's throne is in the highest heaven with Christ Jesus on his right hand while Satan's throne is somewhere at a lower level in the heavenly realm. He rules over his evil spirits there, and together with his spirits he rules this *"present evil age"* of our physical world (**GALATIANS 1:4**).

THE LAND AND THE SEA

When Satan and his evil spirits were cast out of heaven, there was a loud voice in heaven saying:

REVELATION 12: 12
"Therefore rejoice, you heavens and you who dwell in them! But woe to the earth and the sea, because the devil has gone down to you! He is filled with fury, because he knows that his time is short."

1 JOHN 5: 19
"We know... that the whole world is under the control of the evil one"

The evil one in the above scripture is none other but Satan himself. He is bluntly called *"the god of this world"* in **2 CORINTHIANS 4: 4**. The alarming increase in evil and ungodliness in this present physical world is as a result of satanic control over it. When God asked Satan where he was coming from in **JOB 1:7**, he answered: *"I have been going back and forth across the earth, watching everything that's going on"*.

From these regions his evil spiritual kingdom still rules and work against God's will and purpose for mankind.

The great truth to note in this episode is that as there is the spiritual kingdom of God so also there is in existence the satanic spiritual kingdom. Both kingdoms are exercising great influence on our physical world. Many spiritually blind and ignorant people are not aware of this truth.

Chapter Three

THE SPIRITUAL BEGAT THE PHYSICAL

HEBREWS 11: 3
"By faith we understand that the universe was formed at God's command, so that what is seen was not made out of what is visible."

We cannot over emphasize this great truth that life began in the spiritual realm before it ever manifested in the physical realm. Please do not forget this.

God, the Eternal Spirit and King, purposed, according to the riches of His wisdom and for His own glorious pleasure, to create the physical world where He will have a physical set of beings to worship and serve Him, as do the angels in the spiritual realm.

Nobody can query Him for His actions. *"Our God is in heaven;"* says the scripture *"he does whatever pleases him."* (PSALM 115: 3). So in the fullness of time God created the physical world. This is briefly recorded in the book of Genesis.

THE ACT OF CREATION:
GENESIS 1:1.
"In the beginning God created the heavens and the earth."

The word *"heavens"* represent the universe, which God created *"in the beginning"*. Which beginning? Well, we can say the beginning of the creation of the universe.

The scientists have made great discoveries about the universe, many planets apart from the earth have been discovered. These planets are found to be well arranged in a perfect orderly form and people wonder where this universe emerged from. The simple answer is that God, who is the Eternal Spirit, created the heavens and the earth by His word in the beginning.

PSALM 33: 6
"By the word of the LORD were heavens made, their starry host by the breath of his mouth."

We may not be able to say how long this *"beginning"* has been; it could have been several billions of years ago. Only God knows. Whatsoever we know about God is in part (**1 CORINTHIANS 13: 12**).

Scripture also says, *"The secret things belong to the Lord our God, but the things revealed belong to us and to our children forever, that we may follow all the words of this law."* (**DEUTERONOMY 29: 29**). The truth He shows to us in the scripture is enough for us to believe Him. Halleluah!

GENESIS 1:2

"Now the earth was formless and empty, darkness was over the surface of the deep, and the Spirit of God was hovering over the waters."

The word *"Now"* is very significant, it shows that there had been a gap between **GENESIS 1: 1** and **GENESIS 1: 2**. It seems as if, for example, a man had embarked on some project and left it for a long time and suddenly, he came back to the project and said: *"Now I want to continue..."*

The phrase *"now the earth was formless and empty"* shows that God had created the earth in a certain period earlier and there had not been any life on this formless and empty planet earth. We are not sure how long the earth had been in this form. It could have been many billions of years, only God knows.

Further more, the sentence; *"darkness was over the surface of the deep and the Spirit of God was hovering over the waters,"* reveals a tremendous insight to us. It shows that there was no light in the universe at this period in time; it depicts also that the whole shapeless earth was covered with water.

The book of **GENESIS** did not tell us about how God created the water or the darkness, but it just revealed the state of things as at the time God *"came again"* to the earth to do something about it. This shows that the universe, the planet earth, water and darkness had been created at a certain distance time other than the time

God began to decree His word to re-shape the earth in the account of **GENESIS 1:3** downward. This period could have been several billion years earlier.

Here settles one of the major conflicts between the scientists and the Bible scholars. The scientists argue firmly that the planet earth is several billions years of age and thus go against the traditional interpretation of the book of Genesis that the earth is about a few thousand years old. A close study of **GENESIS 1:1** and **2** reveals that possibly the earth could have been in existence for several billions of years ago. There is no disagreement between the Bible and science on this issue.

Before I come back to **GENESIS 1:3** let me go straight to **GENESIS 1:9** which refers to the issue of dry land on planet earth.

GENESIS 1: 9
"And God said, "Let the water under the sky be gathered to one place, and let dry ground appear." And it was so."

A careful observation of this account may also show that God had created the land at the time He created the formless earth. In fact the word *"earth"* means land. This shows that God could have created planet earth formerly comprising land and water but with water covering the surface of the formless earth. Hence in order to put shape to the earth to suit His purpose; in His third day of creation of life in the earth, God commanded the water to gather to one place so that the dry land will appear.

So, when the geologist says that research shows that land has existed for several billions of years, this correlates the account of creation by God and does not in any way negate it.

Going back to **GENESIS 1:3** downward, we see clearly how our God, the Eternal Spirit, put life and shape in process one after the other to the earth. The first day He created the light and separated it from the darkness. Second day He created the sky.

After commanding the dry land to appear from the waters while the waters gathered to one place: *"Then God said, "Let the land produce vegetation; seed - bearing plants and trees on the land that bear fruit with seed in it, according to their various kind." And it was so. The land produced vegetation; plant bearing seeds according to their kinds and trees bearing fruits with seed in it according to their kinds. And God saw that it was good. And there was evening, and there was morning - the third day."* (**GENESIS 11-13**).

The sun, the moon and the stars were created on the fourth day to give illumination to the earth. These three creations are young in the universe no doubt about this, they are literarily the work of the fourth day. Every physical creature in the sea and every bird of the air were created by God's spoken word on the fifth day. All living creatures and various kinds of animals were created on the sixth day.

THE CREATION OF MORTAL MAN

Lastly on that same sixth day of creation:

GENESIS 1:26, 27
"Then God said, "Let us make man in our image, in our likeness, and let them rule over the fish of the sea and the birds of the air, over the life stock, over all the earth, and over all the creatures that move along the ground." So God created man in his own image, in the image of God he created him: male and female he created them."

The physical man is created in the image of the invisible God. What does it mean to be created in the image of God? First, it means our physical body is shaped in the image of God. **GENESIS 2: 7** reveals that it was God Himself who moulded our physical body with clay in His own image. He is our potter.

We can actually imagine it that human beings are shaped like God truly. Various scriptural verses reveals that God also has the parts of the body we have as human beings: He has a head, eyes, mouth, nose, ears, hands and legs. Human beings have not seen exactly into the spiritual realm so we cannot vividly say how this glorious Spirit-God looks like but certainly we are sure that He has some of the parts of our body in the spiritual shapes. He has the spiritual body, we being His image, have the physical body. Below are some of the scriptural verses:

ISAIAH 59: 1
"Surely THE ARM of the LORD is not too short to save, nor HIS EAR too dull to hear."

JEREMIAH 1: 9
"Then the LORD reached out HIS HAND and touched my mouth and said to me, 'Now, I have put my words in your mouth.'"

2 CHRONICLES 16: 9
"For THE EYES of the LORD range throughout the earth to strengthen those whose hearts are fully committed to him."

MALACHI 3:16
"Then those who feared the LORD talked with each other and the LORD listened and heard..."

Let us examine GENESIS 2: 7 closely:

GENESIS 2: 7
"...the Lord God formed the man from the dust of the ground and breathed into His nostrils the breath of life, and the man became a living being."

First, He moulded some clay, then He breathed into its nostrils the breath of life and the man became living as a complete image of God. Both the clay and the breath of God made the complete man.

Through the breath of God virtues were

transferred into man. Scriptures tell us about these virtues: God talks, He has self-will, He thinks and reasons. He is creative, He shows his grievances, love, patience, forgiveness and faithfulness. All these virtues are also in man – this is God's image. God is therefore, the Spirit being with these attributes but we are mortal beings with the same attributes. We are created in His image.

God thus created the natural realm putting the natural man to govern it. The natural realm is lower than the spiritual realm so also the natural human beings are lower than the spirit beings, the angels.

David reveals this truth to us:

PSALM 8:3-9
"When I consider your heavens, the work of your finger's, the moon and the stars, which you have set in place, what is man that you are mindful of him, the son of man that you care for him? You made him a little lower than the heavenly beings and crown him with glory and honour. You made him ruler over the works of your hands; you put everything under his feet: all flocks and herds, and the beasts of the field, and the birds of the air, and the fish of the sea, all that swim and paths of the sea. O LORD, our Lord, how majestic is your name in all the earth!"

Human beings should be grateful to God because we are His handiwork. In the book of Revelation we see how the whole host of heaven renders special songs to God because He created all things for His pleasure.

REVELATION 4: 10, 11; 5:13

"...the twenty-four elders fall down before him who sits on the throne, and worship him who lives ever and ever. They lay their crowns before the throne and say: "You're worthy, our Lord and God, to receive glory and honour and power, for you created all things, and by your will they were created and have their being".... Then I heard every creature in heaven and on earth and under the earth and on the sea, and all that is in them, singing: "To him who sits on the throne and to the Lamb are praise and honour and glory and power, forever and ever!"

THE THREE-FOLD NATURE OF MAN

PSALM 139:14-16

"I praise you because I am fearfully and wonderfully made; your works are wonderful, I know that full well. My frame was not hidden from you when I was made in the secret place. When I was woven together in the depths of the earth, your eyes saw my unformed body."

Human beings are wonderfully and fearfully created. Such knowledge is too wonderful for us to comprehend, it is high, and we cannot attain it, says the psalmist: *"Such knowledge is too wonderful for* me, too lofty for me to attain." (PSALM 139:6).

There is a great mystery in how we were created.

This mystery is evident in what became of man after the spirit of God was breathed into the nostrils of ordinary moulded clay. Bible says, *"And the man became a living soul"* (GENESIS 2: 7 KJV).

The Lord's Spirit has revealed to us from the scriptures that we human beings are made up of three parts.

1 THESSALONIANS 5:23 KJV
"And the very God of peace sanctify you wholly; and I pray God YOUR WHOLE SPIRIT AND SOUL AND BODY be preserved blameless unto the coming of our Lord Jesus Christ."

These parts are spirit, soul and body. In the wisdom of God He has wonderfully created us so.

It is very easy to separate the body from the two others because it is only physical. The spirit and soul are difficult to separate but through the Word of God it can be done.

HEBREWS 4:12
"For the word of God is living and active. Sharper than any double – edged sword, it penetrates even TO DIVIDING SOUL AND SPIRIT, joints and marrow; it judges the thoughts and attitudes of the heart."

In the account of creation in the book of Genesis,

the breath of life which God breathed into the nostrils of ordinary clay did this great wonder. It formed the spirit and the soul; it gave life to the body and confined the spirit and the soul into the body. The three parts thus function together as divinely programmed by the heavenly system software.

"...MAN BECAME A LIVING SOUL":

Soul is man's self-consciousness. He is made conscious of his existence by the work of his soul. It is the seat of our personality. The elements that make us human belong to the soul. Intellect, thoughts, ideas, love, emotions, discernment, choices, decisions, etc are various experiences of the soul.

With the spirit, man can contact the spiritual realm and through the help of his soul he can comprehend what is going on there. Likewise with his body he contacts the physical realm and through the help of his soul he can understand what is going on here.

The physical man is like a double creature able to contact the spiritual and the physical realms.

But, why did God create us this way? He did it so that we can relate with Him being a spirit being (only spirit can relate with spirit), and also that we may relate with the physical world. This was the original state man was in the garden of Eden before the fall, thus God came in the cool of the day to fellowship with man. Although man is permitted to have insight into the spiritual realm, he is however, mainly designed by the creator to function in the physical realm. So he is more familiar with the physical realm than the spiritual.

Spiritual death came on man finally when Satan, the evil spirit being, superimposed himself on a natural being, the snake, to deceive mankind. Hence man became absolutely conscious of the natural realm and its principles. Satan introduced man to his evil spiritual kingdom. Virtually the whole world began to worship the devil and all his fallen angels.

Jesus has redeemed us now. Once again we can understand the spiritual realm, perceive what goes on there and once in a while be permitted by God to catch the glimpse of it. How? Through the Holy Spirit of God given to us who are "born again". Our spirits as Christians are now born again and able to fellowship with God.

But the fact is that the spirit is still housed in the physical body. Man naturally is used to the physical realm than the spiritual. This is why God requires us as Christians to walk by faith. *"...blessed is the man who do not see and yet believe"* (JOHN 20:29).

CHAPTER FOUR

MOVEMENTS IN THE SPIRITUAL REALM |

Angels and demons, being the spirit creatures, are mainly the ones who move about in the spiritual realm. They have considerably very fast speed than the fastest jet or spacecraft ever made by man. As discussed earlier, these angels are of two categories: some set for God and others for Satan. Both groups are always in conflicts whenever they meet. There are several scriptural texts based on this, let us consider few of them.

Angel Gabriel was sent by God to give an answer to Daniel's prayers in a city called Persia; the angel travelled from heaven to earth in the realm of the spirit, on getting to the spiritual border of Persia, **"the prince of the Persian Kingdom,"** who was the satanic angel in charge of that city, arrested and detained Gabriel, the angel sent by God. God had to send another archangel, Michael, to rescue angel Gabriel. He narrated the story to Daniel when he eventually got to him:

Daniel. 10: 12, 13, 20

"Then he (Gabriel) continued, "do not be afraid, Daniel. Since the first day that you set your mind to gain understanding and to humble yourself before your God, your words were heard, and I have come in response to them. But the prince of the Persian kingdom resisted me twenty – one days. Then Michael, one of the chief princes, came to help me, because I was detained there with the king of Persia...Do you know why I have come to you? Soon I will return to fight against the prince of Persia..."

You notice the word *"prince"* used in the scriptures above, the angels refer to themselves as princes because they are also called the sons of God, and they know God as their Eternal King. The rebellious angels who followed Satan are also referred to as princes. That is why angel Gabriel called both Michael and Satan's angel princes. We also see Jesus referring to Satan as prince in JOHN 14: 30, this is because the Lord was showing us that Satan himself was one of the chief princes of God before he rebelled, after which, according to the Lord Jesus, he became the prince of this world.

John 14: 30

"...for the prince of this world is coming. He has no hold on me,..."

Let us consider one more example, in JUDE 1: 18 we read that:

JUDE 1: 18
"But even the archangel Michael, when he was disputing with the devil about the body of Moses, did not dare to bring a slanderous accusation against him, but he said "the Lord rebuke you!"

Angels fight in the realm of the spirit up till now. Let me give you one practical example, a Christian could pray just as we saw Daniel did and an angel may be sent to give the answer, and an evil angel from the accuser of the brethren, the Satan, could resist the angel of God saying that the person whom the message is sent to is not worthy of it because of one sin or the other in such person's life. Many answers to prayers are delayed in this manner. As we run away from sins, giving no ground for the devil to accuse us, then we will know that no evil spirit can hinder our prayers in Jesus name.

DIFFERENCES BETWEEN GOD'S ANGELS AND SATAN'S

I quickly want to point out some differences between God's angels and Satan's as revealed in the scriptures.

God's angels can come to people in the form of human beings but they do not possess human beings. One good example from the scriptures is in the book of **JUDGES 13**, the angel of the Lord appeared to Samson's mother in the form of a man of God and foretold Samson's birth.

Judges 13: 6 – 10

"Then the woman went to her husband and told him, 'A MAN OF GOD CAME TO ME. He looked like an angel of God, very awesome. I didn't ask him where he came from, and he didn't tell me his name. But he said to me, 'You will conceive and give birth to a son. Now then, drink no wine or other fermented drink and do not eat anything unclean, because the boy will be a nazirite of God from birth until the day of his death.' Then Manoah prayed to the LORD: 'O Lord, I beg you, let THE MAN OF GOD you sent to us come again to teach us how to bring up the boy who is to be born.' God heard Manoah, and THE ANGEL OF GOD came again to the woman while she was out in the field; but her husband Manoah was not with her. The woman hurried to tell her husband, 'He's here! The man who appeared to me the other day!' "

It was when the angel ascended in the flame of fire in their presence that they realised he was an angel of God.

In the same manner, in Genesis 18, three angels were sent from God in the form of human beings to give messages to Abraham about the birth of Isaac and the destruction of Sodom and Gomorrah. This is why as Christians we are commanded in the scripture to give ourselves to hospitality, for in so doing we might be entertaining angels without knowing (**HEBREWS 13: 2**).

You may ask, *"Do you say angels can still come to the world today in the form of human beings?"* The answer is yes! Otherwise God's word will not have commanded us to do it. We as Christians are called to understand spiritual truths and principles.

On the contrary, Satan and all his evil spirits seek to possess human beings, if given the chance, in order to manipulate them for evil activities. The devil himself possessed Judas Iscariot, the disciple who betrayed the Lord Jesus.

JOHN 13: 2, 27
"The evening meal was being served, and the devil had already prompted Judas Iscariot, Son of Simon, to betray Jesus…As soon as Judas took the bread, Satan entered into him."

The Bible says the devil had already prompted Judas, this implies that he had already inspired him in his mind to betray Jesus. Judas could have refused to yield to the temptation of the devil but he chose to yield. This is the same way devil got Eve in the Garden of Eden to sin; he has not changed his method. Finally the Bible says, *"Satan entered him."*

He did not send any other demon to possess Judas because no demon could stand before Jesus. Satan himself was the one who did the possession of Judas just to trap Jesus. We all must understand this.

The mad man of Gadara is another good example to show us that Satan and his evil spirits do possess human beings:

MARK 5: 1, 2, 6-9
"They went across the lake to the region of the Gerasenes. When Jesus got out of the boat, a man with an evil spirit came from the tombs to meet him...When he saw Jesus from a distance, he ran and fell on his kneels in front of him. He shouted at the top of his voice, "What do you want with me, Jesus, Son of the Most High God? Swear to God that you won't torture me!" For Jesus had said to him, "come out of this man, you evil spirit!" Then Jesus asked him, "What is your name?" "My name is legion," he replied, "for we are many."

We must understand that all strong occultists are possessed with strong demons and with many other demons on errand for them.

The devil can put thoughts into man's mind and cause man to think evil, even a Christian who is not very careful can fall victim. We should learn from Ananias and Sapphira, the Christian couple who allowed the devil to instigate them to lie to the minister of God. (**ACTS 5: 1 - 11**).

Men can see the visions of angels (**LUKE 24:22, 23**). The vision can either be from God's angels or Satan's. To safeguard ourselves, any prophetic experiences, visions or dream must be judged by the word of God.

1 JOHN 4:1-3
"Dear friends, do not believe every spirit, but trust the spirit to see whether they're from God, because many false prophets have gone out into the world."

The Bible warns us that the activities of the devil will increase in the last days (**1 TIMOTHY 4:1-3**). Lying signs and wonders will be performed by the demons to mislead the world.

2 CORINTHIANS 11:14-15
"And no wonder, for Satan himself masquerades as an angel of light. It is not surprising, then, if his servants masquerades as servants of righteousness. Their end will be what their actions deserve."

We must therefore be cautious by staying close to the truth – God's Word.

HUMANS' SPIRITS

Apart from the angels and demons, humans' spirits also travel in the realm of the spirit. This may sound unbelievable to many, but it is true.

The human spirit can travel in the spiritual realm in two ways: when the material body is dead, and when the spirit-man is projected out of the body while the material body is not yet dead. **CHAPTERS 6** and **7** of this book provide detailed explanation as regards this; please take time to read it.

LAW OF UTTERANCES

Spoken words are very strong in the realm of the spirit. God does not joke with spoken words neither does the devil. Every spirit being respects utterances.

God's word set things in motion both in spiritual and physical realms; when He speaks the angels move at His command to carry out what His word says, the earth also responds to His words. The word of God has a dynamic and mysterious power in the spiritual realm to cause things to happen even without the help of any angel. Similarly, Satan's words are carried out by his evil angels and demons.

These angels manipulate the physical world also to respond to their spiritual instructions.

When there are no utterances, that is, the message, angels, both God's and Satan's do not move; they only move at the command of the spoken words. The Bible is full of examples of this truth. In the account of the creation in **GENESIS 1: 3**, God spoke, *"let there be light"* instantly the universe responded to that utterance, *"and there was light."*

This is an instance of the potency of God's word without the help of any angel.

Another instance is the account in **LUKE 1: 26, 27** where *"...God sent angel Gabriel to Nazareth, a town in Galilee, to a virgin pledged to be married to a man named Joseph, a descendant of David. This virgin's name was Mary."* This is the testimony about the birth of Jesus Christ.

I just want you to get the revelation that the spoken words are powerful in the realm of the spirit; and be it an utterance from God, Satan or man; it is the main cause of movements there in. In other words when there is no spoken message, then there is no movement in the spirit realm.

DELIVERANCE

I always use this principle in the course of deliverance. During a particular deliverance session, we commanded the demon to get out of a sister, and he replied us through the mouth of that sister, *"I am sent on errand into her life, I am obeying the order..."* Instantly, I understood this spiritual principle. I asked, *"What is the spoken message you are acting upon, and who sent you into her life?"* The demon explained every detail. We knew the origin of his message, it was from the devil. Now, I had to deal with the message, the messenger and the source of the message as this would make the sister to become free from this demonic oppression.

Then I said, *"You are sent with evil utterances but I speak as the oracle of God..."* (I pronounced the words of God from my mouth to nullify the evil words that had been spoken). I cried out, *"I nullify these evil utterances in the name of Jesus."* Then I spoke to the demon, *"no more message to keep you working in her life, therefore you have no right to stay in her again"* he said, *"yes I know"*. We released the spoken words of God against the source of every evil utterance, and cast out the demon, and he fled! Then knowing fully well that our own utterances also command attention in the realm of the spirit as the oracles of God (1 PETER 4: 11), we released utterances of restoration and blessing into the life of that sister. Thank God she is doing fine in the Lord till now.

BELIEVER'S AUTHORITY

Men of God and all the children of God who understand spiritual principles and their position in Christ have authority to rebuke satanic utterances and to release God's words through their own utterances into the spirit realm. *"What next?"* you may ask, just relax God and the angels will take care of the rest. Remember the incident in the book of Joshua after the fall of the wall of Jericho:

JOSHUA 1: 26
"At that time Joshua pronounced this solemn oath: "Cursed before the LORD is the man who undertakes to rebuild this city, Jericho: At the cost of his firstborn son will he lay the

foundations; at the cost of his youngest will he set up its gates."

Joshua, who knew his position in God released the spoken words into the realm of the spirit, forgot about it and left the rest to God. Notice that he said *"cursed before the LORD..."* God took it as His own word and began to watch over it for its performance.

He says in JEREMIAH 1: 12, *"...for I am watching to see that my word is fulfilled."* Do not forget He also says in ISAIAH 44: 26 that He is the Lord *"who carries out the words of his servants and fulfils the predictions of his messengers."*

In the physical nothing serious happened after the utterance was pronounced by Joshua, yet in the spiritual realm it had been taken very seriously. Let me repeat this that there is no joking in the realm of the spirit about utterances.

About 530 years later, after the death of Joshua, the Bible tells us that a certain man rose up to rebuild the wall of Jericho:

1 KINGS 16: 34
"In Ahab's time, Hiel of Bethel rebuilt Jericho. He laid the foundations at the cost of his first Abiram, and he set up its gates at the cost of his youngest son Segub, in accordance with the word of the LORD spoken by Joshua the son of Nun."

I want you to notice the last line of the scripture

above, it says, ***"in accordance with the word of the LORD spoken by Joshua..."*** That utterance spoken by Joshua is regarded as the word of God Himself.

This is to show you that the word of God is spoken through the men of God. Do not forget this. God cannot come down to speak to your life, His words are in the mouth of His ministers, He takes their words as His own words and will not deny its fulfilments.

Let us study the situation of this man, it was either he never knew anyone had spoken against the rebuilt of Jericho or he heard about it from people who kept the records and yet deliberately counted it as irrelevant. Yet, as he ventured to rebuild it, the spiritual realm moved to fulfil the utterance spoken long ago. Whether it was an angel who killed his sons or not we do not know but we know that their deaths came from the realm of the spirit. This insensitive man truncated the lives of his innocent children. This is the same way today that many people fall or become victims of utterances, which has, in one way or the other, been released into the realm of the spirit.

This principle works, whether in curses or blessing, from the devil or God, from God's ministers or Satan's ministers; it is all the same spiritual principle.

Length of time is not a barrier to the fulfilment of any utterance spoken in the spiritual realm. If a curse has been released into the spiritual realm about somebody or something, it will continue to work from generation to generation until God's word is spoken to cancel it. This is a very important spiritual principle.

WHAT HAPPENS WHEN WE PRAY?

Prayer is both a spiritual principle as well as physical one. It is a natural action we as human beings take, which simultaneously brings God into a corresponding supernatural or spiritual action.

Are you yearning to contact God? Then learn to pray. There is nowhere a sincere prayer is said without God coming to respond to such prayers.

Many times when we pray, we don't know what transpires in the spirit realm. When we receive our answers, we can't comprehend how God did it, and all we do is praise Him for it.

Through the Holy Spirit, the scripture opens our eyes of understanding to see some actions, which occur in the realm of the spirit when Christians pray:

God may send angels to respond to the prayers. For example, the angel of God was sent to respond to Hezekiah's prayer in **ISAIAH CHAPTER 37**. Angel Gabriel was also sent in response to Daniel's prayers in **DANIEL CHAPTER 10**.

When the church prayed for Peter in **ACTS**

CHAPTER 12, the angel of the Lord was sent to rescue Peter from the prison. There are a lot of examples in the scripture, which shows that God can send his angels to respond to the prayer of His children.

HEBREWS 1:14
"Are not all angels ministering spirits sent to serve those who will inherit salvation?"

Apart from angels, we should know that God's word works alone. All creatures hear God and He can influence and control any of His creatures directly.

Let's take some examples: Jesus prayed to stop the storm and the storm heard Him. His disciples saw it and exclaimed, *"...Who is this? Even the wind and the waves obey him!"* (**MARK 4:41**).

Also in **MARK 11**, Jesus' prayer dried up a tree. Peter's prayer raised the dead (**ACTS 9: 40**). Elijah's prayer caused both fire and rain to fall from heaven. Moses prayed and the ground opened up, and so on.

When we pray, ours is not to know which way is convenient for God to answer. He may decide to use angels, situations, or put thoughts in man, that is not our own business. All we know is that He will answer us and we will glorify Him.

He may answer exactly the way we prayed, He may need to arrange or re-arrange events to cause our answers to come, in which we need to exercise patience, but eventually He will glorify Himself.

There are some principles in the Bible that are given to us by God to guide us concerning prayers:

1 JOHN 5:14, 15

"This is the confidence we have in approaching God: that if we ask anything according to his will, he hears us. And if we know that he hears us – whatever we ask – we know that we have what we ask of him."

JEREMIAH 33: 3

"Call unto me and I will answer you and tell you great and unsearchable things you do not know."

PHILIPPIANS 4: 6

"Do not be anxious about anything, but in everything, by prayer and petition, with thanks giving, present your request to God."

MARK 11:24, 25

"Therefore I tell you, whatever you ask for in prayer, believe that you have received it, and it will be yours. And when you stand praying, if you hold anything against anyone, forgive him, so that your Father in heaven may forgive your sins."

HEBREWS 10: 35, 36

"So do not throw away your confidence; it will be richly rewarded. You need to persevere so that when you have done the will of God, you will receive what he has promised."

CHAPTER FIVE

THIS COMPLICATED WORLD

We should seek to get the revelation knowledge of this present world in which we live. The scientists have tried and are still helping tremendously to discover so many things in this world. Thank God for giving them this wisdom.

However there is a limitation to their understanding of this world in that they are operating only in the physical realm. Most of the modern scientists, except few who are Christian among them, do not have insight into the spiritual realities because they are spiritually dead and insensitive. This is one of the strategies of the devil, the god of this present evil age.

2 CORINTHIANS 4:4
"The god of this age blinded the minds of the unbelievers, so that they cannot see the light of the gospel of the glory of Christ, who is the image of God."

What are the various beings co-existing in this present evil world?

Human beings were originally the legal residents of this earth.

PSALM 115: 16
"**The highest heavens belong to the LORD, but the earth he has given to man.**"

Due to the fall of man Satan and his evil angels also gained entrance into this world. When God asked Satan where he was coming from in **JOB 1:7** he replied: "*...I have been going back and forth across the earth, watching everything that's going on.*"

In the book of **REVELATION**, the Bible also reveals that Satan and his evil angels were hurled down to the earth:

REVELATION 12:12
"**Therefore rejoice, you heavens and you who dwell in them! But woe to the earth and the sea, because the devil has gone down to you! He is filled with fury, because he knows that his time is short.**"

Satan introduced and deepened mankind into all sorts of evil acts including various sins and the worship of demons. Human being on earth thus formed two major categories: **Ordinary people** and **Evil spiritual people**. The ordinary people seek guidance from evil spiritual people under the satanic directions. Those who practise witchcraft, sorcery, spiritists, various idol priests and all evil religions priests are in this category of **Evil spiritual people**.

Under the direction of demons they enslave people, torture them and even kill them for various satanic sacrifices. Their victims also being enslaved to Satan through sin do not know the way out.

Then, out of great darkness the light of God shone into the world. God our creator, according to the riches of His mercy, sent His only begotten Son to the world to die for our sins so that the world would be delivered from the grip of Satan and his demons.

COLOSSIANS 1:13, 14
"For he has rescued us from the dominion of darkness and brought us into the kingdom of the Son he loves, in whom we have redemption, the forgiveness of sins."

Those who believe in the Son of God, the Lord Jesus Christ, are rescued from darkness back to light. They are called Christians, **The Heavenly Spiritual People**. Satan cannot defeat them. They are the warriors sent by the Lord Jesus to preach the gospel of God's kingdom so as to rescue others from the grip of Satan's claw.

GOD'S SPIRIT AND HEAVENLY HOSTS ARE HERE:

The presence of Christians in this world makes God to dwell in the world today. Jesus Christ is now reigning amidst His enemies. The Holy Spirit of God is in the world operating in individual Christians in the church and the body of Christ at large, resisting the works of the devils and cooperating with the saints to win souls into the kingdom of God.

JOHN 14: 16, 17
"And I will ask the father, and he will give you another Counsellor to be with you forever – the Spirit of truth. The world cannot accept him, because it neither sees him nor knows him. But you know him, for he lives with you and will be in you."

Also, the heavenly angels are all around here on earth. They do not stay on earth but go to and fro the heaven and earth as messengers of all the children of God. They are always in combat with the evil angels.

JOHN 1: 51
"He (Jesus) then added, "I tell you the truth, you shall see heaven open, and the angels of God ascending and descending on the Son of Man"

HEBREWS 1: 14
"Are not all angels ministering spirits sent to serve those who will inherit salvation?"

This present world is a Battle Zone. It is more complicated than I have lightly summarised here. This is just to give us understanding so that we should not be ignorant of where we dwell. In the preceding chapter we shall fully discuss the effect of Satan's control over this present age.

Insight Into THE SPIRITUAL REALM |

CHAPTER SIX

WHAT HAPPENS WHEN A MAN DIES? |

The spirit of man does not die like all other spirit beings in the realm of the spirit. When a natural man dies, it means that the physical body has expired or stopped working, instantly the spirit-man having the soul is separated from the body and live on in the realm of the spirit. It goes either to God in paradise or to torment in hell. The parable of the Rich man and Lazarus is a good illustration of this.

LUKE 16: 22 - 31

"The time came when the beggar died and the angels carried him to Abraham's side. The rich man also died and was buried. In hell, where he was in torment, he looked up and saw Abraham far away, with Lazarus by his side. So he called to him, 'Father Abraham, have pity on me and send Lazarus to dip the tip of his finger in water and cool my tongue, because I am in agony in this fire.' But Abraham replied, 'Son, remember that in your lifetime you received your good things, while Lazarus received bad things, but now he is comforted here but you are in agony.

And besides all these, between us and you a great chasm has been fixed, so that those who want to go from here to you cannot, nor can anyone cross over from there to us.' He answered, ' then I beg you, father, send Lazarus to my father's house, for I have five brother's .Let him warn them, so that they will not also come to this place of torment.' Abraham replied, 'They have Moses and the Prophets; let them listen to them.' ' No, father Abraham,' He said, ' but if someone from the dead goes to them, they will repent.' he said to him, ' If they do not listen to Moses and the Prophets, they will not be convinced if someone rises from the dead.'"

Notice that the three people mentioned are very much alive with their senses retained but not with their physical bodies, for the body is dead already. The spirit-man of the individual mentioned was alive in the realm of the spirit. This is what happens to anyone who died in this world.

There was also another brother in the book of ACTS, Stephen, who was actually stoned to death by the rebels but at the point of death he said certain things:

ACTS 7:56 - 60

"'Look,' he (Stephen) said, 'I SEE HEAVEN OPEN AND THE SON OF MAN STANDING AT THE RIGHT HAND OF GOD.'... While they were stoning him, Stephen prayed, 'LORD JESUS, RECEIVE MY

SPIRIT.' Then he fell on his knees and cried out, 'Lord, do not hold this sin against them.' When he had said this, he fell asleep."

Testimony

Let me briefly share the experience with you of a sister I will call Kate (she testified herself in the church). She had been sick for a couple of weeks until this particular night when her situation detoriated. At mid-night she perceived a cold breeze blow over her body, lifting her up and suspending her in the air. Then the breeze blew her out of the house.

She noticed that, there was her body on the bed lying lifelessly, yet she could see another of "herself" outside glancing at her own body on the bed, her husband was also lying on the bed. She also noticed that there was a force that held her down outside and turned her attention to the inner room. Although there was a wall that obscured the view of a physical person from seeing what was going on inside, she observed that she could clearly see through the wall and it was not a barrier at all.

Suddenly, she saw her husband screaming and vigorously shaking her lifeless body on the bed; she was agitated but could do nothing about it. This continued for some minutes then, there came another warm breeze, which blew her back into the house and into the lifeless body on the bed. Suddenly she woke up, screamed in fear and narrated to her husband what had happened. She came to the church to tell everybody her experience and then made a commitment to serve the Lord all her life for the Lord had shown her that there is life after death.

We Christians know that to die is gain. Our absence in the world is to be present with the Lord Jesus Christ in the spiritual planet of heaven. Anybody who dies as a sinner will have his or her spirit-man cast to hell and shall partake in the second death, the lake of fire (**REVELATION 20: 20**).

PARADISE OR HELL

When the Lord Jesus Christ was hanging on the cross, He said to the thief who repented at the point of death:

LUKE 23:43
"Jesus answered him, 'I tell you the truth, today you will be with me in paradise'"

Also in his parable of the Rich man and Lazarus cited earlier, although very poor while on earth, Lazarus a righteous man died. The rich man who was unrighteous also died and both were buried. To many whenever someone dies and is buried, for such we say it is over. But in the realm of the spirit it is the beginning of a new journey. After the physical death, the angels of God accompanied the spirit-man of Lazarus to Abraham's bosom. The spirit-man of the rich man was sent to hell. Abraham said to the rich man in hell when he asked for a drop of water to cool himself down:

LUKE 16: 25
"But Abraham replied, Son, remember that in your life time you received your good things, while Lazarus received bad things, but now he is comforted here and you are in agony."

Paradise is a place of comfort and rest. Whenever a Christian dies physically we offer a prayer at the burial ground that *"may his/her soul rest in peace"* because we know that our brethren who died are going to be with the Lord in paradise.

What about hell? It is a place of torment; in **LUKE 16:23** the Bible says that the rich man was in torment in hell. He cried in **VERSE 24**, *"Because I am in agony in this fire"*. He finally begged Abraham in **VERSE 27**, *"Then I beg you, Father, send Lazarus to my father's house for I have five brothers. 'Let him warn them, so that they will not also come to this place of torment.' Abraham replied, 'They have Moses and the Prophets; let them listen to them.' ' No , father Abraham ,' He said , ' but if someone from the dead goes to them , they will repent .' he said to him , ' If they do not listen to Moses and the Prophets , they will not be convinced if someone rises from the dead .'"*

Christians are the Moses and the Prophets of this generation. Let us warn the sinners of the impending doom awaiting anyone who rejects the salvation of Christ Jesus.

Apostle Peter's Teaching

One of the hard saying in the Bible is this issue of hell for sinners. Many religious cults have bluntly rejected the existence of hell as a place of torment. They reduced hell to mean just a grave and nothing more. Apostle Peter, thank God for his life, gave us a great insight into the spiritual realm most especially in this case, about hell:

2 Peter 2:4
"For if God did not spare angels when they sinned, but sent them to hell, putting them into gloomy dungeon to be held for judgement."

We saw clearly here that the angels, which are spirit beings and not mortal like us, when they sinned, God sent them to hell. So here hell is a place of torment for spirits and it is a gloomy dungeon where God chained these disobedient spirit beings.

Hell is not a permanent eternal place where the disobedient spirit beings will be punished, but they are to be held there for the judgement day. The day of judgement will come, the spirits in hell, both of angels and humans will be judged by God and sentenced to the lake of fire, which is the second death. This is the eternal punishment.

Matthew 25:41
"Then he will say to those on his left, 'Depart from me, you who are cursed, INTO

ETERNAL FIRE PREPARED FOR THE DEVIL AND HIS ANGELS.'"

REVELATION .20: 10-15
"And the devil, who deceived them, was thrown INTO THE LAKE OF BURNING SULPHUR, WHERE THE BEAST AND THE FALSE PROPHETS HAD BEEN THROWN. THEY WILL BE TORMENTED DAY AND NIGHT FOR EVER AND EVER. Then I saw a great white throne and him who was seated on it. Earth and sky fled from his presence, and there was no place for them. And I saw the dead, great and small, standing before the throne, and books were opened. Another book was opened, which is the book of life. The dead were judged according to what they had done as recorded in the books. The sea gave up the dead that were in it and death and Hades (Hell) gave up the dead that were in them and each person was judged according to what he had done. Then death and Hades (Hell) were thrown into the lake of fire. The lake of fire is the second death. IF ANYONE'S NAME WAS NOT FOUND WRITTEN IN THE BOOK OF LIFE, HE WAS THROWN INTO THE LAKE OF FIRE."

Note VERSE **14** of the above scripture, *'Then death and Hades (Hell) were thrown into the lake of fire. The lake of fire is the second death.'*

After the judgement of the world of sinners, there will not be death again hence no more need for prison-hell. So God cast both death and hell into the lake of fire. Christians who are faithful to God will not partake in this terrible judgement for rapture would have taken place earlier and we would have been with the Lord enjoying – Halleluiah!

JESUS PREACHED TO SPIRITS IN HELL

1 PETER 3:18-20...4:5,6 NLT

"Christ also suffered when he died for our sins once for all time. He never sinned, but he died for sinners that he might bring us safely home to God. He suffered physical death, but he was raised to life in the Spirit. So he went and preached to the spirits in prison – those who disobeyed God long ago when God waited patiently while Noah was building his boat. Only eight people were saved from the drowning in that terrible flood.... But just remember that they will have to face God, who will judge everyone, both the living and the dead. That is why the Good news was preached even to those who have died – so that although their bodies were punished with death, they could still live in the spirit as God does."

When the Lord Jesus Christ died on the cross physically the Bible says:

LUKE 23:46
"Jesus called out with a loud voice, 'Father, into your hands I commit my spirit.'" When he had said this, he breathed his last."

His mortal body was buried quite alright; all His accusers and crucifiers thought it was over because they knew nothing about life after death. Apostle Peter tells us that *"he suffered physical death, but he was raised to life in the spirit"*. Jesus' spirit was very active in the realm of the spirit even though His body was dead. The Bible says He went to hell; that prison, to preach. Someone might say, *"Did I hear you say Jesus went to hell?"* Yes! God's word is showing it to us all. The Lord went to hell to preach the good news to the human spirits who disobeyed since the time of Noah.

This further shows that those who died physically on earth before Jesus Christ came were alive in the spirit. Jesus Christ between His death and resurrection went to preach to those human spirits.

Let us further check the account of Matthew on what happened when Jesus Christ died:

MATTHEW 27: 50-53
"And when Jesus had cried out again in aloud voice, he gave up his spirit. At that moment the curtain of the temple was torn in two from top to bottom. The earth shook and the rocks split. The tombs broke open and the bodies of many holy people who had died were raised to life. They came out of the tombs, and after Jesus'

resurrection they went into the holy city and appeared to many people."

Some may say, *"This is impossible!"* Well, thank God because He is the only wise one. Secret things belong to Him alone, whatever He reveals to us is what we know (**DEUTERONOMY. 29:29**). The issue of salvation is deeper than what we can fully grasp. No human can fully comprehend the things in the spiritual realm while he lives in this earthly tent of the body. Apostle Paul, who is well respected about the revelation of the spiritual realm clearly stated: *"...Now I know in part; then I shall know fully, even I am fully known."* (1 CORINTHIANS.13: 12)

When we get to heaven we shall see clearly but now we walk by faith. All glory be to God!

OUR BODY- THE EARTHLY TENT

Apostle Peter made a very clear statement to us:

2 PETER 1:12-15

"So I will always remind you of these things, even though you know them and are firmly established in the truth you now have. I think it is right to refresh your memory AS LONG AS I LIVE IN THE TENT OF THIS BODY, BECAUSE I KNOW THAT I WILL SOON PUT IT ASIDE, as our Lord Jesus Christ has made clear to me. And I will make every effort to see that after my departure you will always be able to remember these things."

He was getting to the end of his earthly ministry and was lead to write this epistle for us so that we will continue to understand the things of the spirit of God.

First of all, he was not afraid of death because the Lord has shown him that he would soon die a physical death. Christians need not be afraid of physical death because it is an entrance into eternity with the Lord Jesus Christ. The Lord Jesus Christ, though no more in His physical body, is still very much alive forever more in the realm of the spirit. He declared boldly in **REVELATION 1:18**: *"I am the Living One; I was dead, and behold I am alive for ever and ever! And I hold the keys of death and Hades."*

We also noticed that Apostle Peter said, *"...as long as I live in the tent of this body, because I know that I will soon put it aside..."* He was living in the body as at the time of writing this epistle but he was going to come out of the body. When he comes out he would still continue to live in the spirit realm although the body would have died.

Apostle Paul reveals the same truth to us:

PHILIPPIANS 1: 21-25

"For to me, to live is Christ and to die is gain. IF I AM TO GO ON LIVING IN THE BODY, this will mean fruitful labor for me. Yet what shall I choose? I do not know! I am torn between the two: I DESIRE TO DEPART AND BE WITH CHRIST, which is better by far; but it is more necessary for you that I REMAIN IN THE

BODY. Convinced of this, I know that I will remain, and I will continue with all of you for your progress and joy in the faith."

The word, *"I"* both used by Peter and Paul in these scriptural texts above mean the real Peter and Paul, their *"spirit-man"* and not their physical bodies at all. Paul could live in the tent of the physical body or could come out of the body and ***"depart to be with Christ"*** in the realm of the spirit to be with the Lord *"which is far better"*. When he comes out of the body, the body becomes dead and no option than to bury it. This is called the physical death.

This physical body in its present corrupt form is just a tent where we live temporarily. The time is coming when Christ will transform this our mortal body to the glorious immortal one. That will be at the time of rapture. (**1 CORINTHIANS 15:42-44; 1 THESSALONIANS 3:15-17; ROMANS 8: 23**).

Many people in the world, Christians inclusive, are ignorant of this truth so they live as if life is all about this physical body. Apostle Paul warns us:

2 CORINTHIANS 5: 10
"For we must all appear before the judgement seat of Christ, that each one may receive what is due to him for the things done WHILE IN THE BODY, whether good or bad."

While you are in this body, be careful, for whatever you do is in the heavenly records in the realm of the spirit – you will give account either good or bad.

CHAPTER SEVEN

THE SPIRIT-MAN'S EXPERIENCES OUTSIDE THE BODY |

The things of the spirit are naturally very difficult to comprehend for a natural man, yet it is worth given keen attention to because of its eternal value unlike the things of the physical realm, which is just temporal (**2 CORINTHIANS. 4: 18**).

Let us ask ourselves some questions again. What happens when a spirit leaves the material body? We have seen in our study earlier that when someone dies here on earth, the spirit of such person comes out of the body retaining its consciousness. If he is a Christian the angels of God accompanies him to the paradise in heaven. We have seen Stephen in **ACTS 7**, at the point of death God opened his spiritual eyes to see the Lord Jesus Christ rising up from the throne in heaven ready to welcome his spirit-man to heaven. Then on seeing this Stephen cried, *"Lord accept my spirit"* then he died.

If the person is an unbeliever, the one who reject the gospel of salvation, he is ushered to hell, a prison full of darkness and torment of fire; he is reserved there until the final day of judgement. We also saw the unrighteous rich man in hell where he cried, *"I am in torment in this fire"*. These two cases are after death experiences of the spirit-man.

Let us divert into another area now. Is it possible for the spirit-man of a person to leave the body while that person is not yet dead? If it is possible, then, how? What is going to be the experience of that spirit in the spiritual realm? What is going to happen to the material body when the spirit is left? How will the spirit-man come back to the body again? When the spirit-man comes back to the body is he going to be conscious that he has been outside the body? Will he remember the experience while out of the body? These are some of the numerous questions this topic generates. Well, let us search the scripture together for the truth about this issue.

I want us to study the spiritual experiences of three great men of God from the scripture, one in the Old Testament and two in the New Testament. These men had such a glorious spiritual experiences that will answer some of the questions above.

PROPHET EZEKIEL - THE TRAVELLING PROPHET

EZEKIEL 8: 1-3

"In the sixth year, in the sixth month on the fifth day, while I was sitting in my house and the elders of Judah were sitting before me, the hand of the Sovereign LORD came upon me there. I looked, and I saw a figure like that of a man. From what appeared to be his waist down he was like fire, and from there up his appearance was as bright as glowing metal. **HE STRETCHED OUT WHAT LOOKED LIKE A HAND AND TOOK ME BY THE HAIR OF MY HEAD. THE SPIRIT LIFTED ME UP BETWEEN EARTH AND HEAVEN AND IN VISIONS OF GOD HE TOOK ME TO JERUSALEM,** to the entrance to the north gate of the inner court, where the idol that provokes to jealousy stood."

I called this man a travelling prophet because he travelled in the realm of the spirit to so many places while his body stayed in a particular physical location. Considering the text above, this man was together with the leaders of Judah in his house. He was in his house physically when suddenly the Holy Spirit came in form of fire and brightness to him. First, God opened his spiritual eyes to see, he said: *"I looked, and I saw..."* Other people in the house with him did not see or feel anything, yet the glorious presence of the Lord was already in the house.

In our Christian meetings the man of God may rise up to say something like, " ***the awesome glory of God is in this place***" yet a natural man, even the Christian whose spiritual eyes God has not opened nor has grown to this level of spiritual understanding will not see or understand. All things may seem ordinary and normal and many people tend to doubt or even not take it seriously and thus miss their blessing.

We must understand that God will not always open our spiritual eyes, and that is why He has made provision for our spiritual understanding so that we may comprehend the spiritual things and principles, and thus urged us to live by faith. Has the Lord Jesus not said that, *"Where two or three are gathered in my name there I am?"* So as for me I always know by faith that God is present in our gatherings.

Prophet Ezekiel said, *"I looked, and I saw..."* This is one level of spiritual vision in which God just opened the eyes of His ministers to see into the spiritual realm. God talks to many of His children in this form; for example, He opened the spiritual eyes of Apostle Peter to see in a vision, a plate containing various kinds of four-footed animals, reptiles and birds descending from heaven (**ACTS 10:9**). During this vision Peter was conscious that he was in a house.

But the vision of prophet Ezekiel transcends this level because he did not only see the vision but the Holy Spirit called his spirit-man out of his body. *"The Spirit lift me up between earth and heaven and in visions of God ..."* The Holy Spirit took his spirit-man out to show him many things in many places in Jerusalem, and also to tell him many secret things.

EZEKIEL 11:1

"Then the Spirit lifted me up and brought me to the gate the house of the LORD that face east..."

This sounds so unbelievable to some people, but it was true. Ezekiel's spirit-man was travelling all over the places with the Holy Spirit yet his physical body was still in his house sub-consciously.

EZEKIEL 11: 24,25

"THE SPIRIT LIFTED ME UP AND BROUGHT ME TO THE EXILES IN BABYLONIA in the vision given by the Spirit of God. Then the vision I had seen went up from me, AND I TOLD THE EXILES EVERYTHING THE LORD HAD SHOWN ME."

At the end of the vision the Holy Spirit brought him back to Babylon, in his house, and back to his material body. He then became conscious of everything that had happened and narrated everything to his people. What a spiritual experience!

APOSTLE PAUL CAUGHT UP INTO PARADISE

2 CORINTHIANS 12:2-4 NLT

"I was caught up into third heaven fourteen years ago. Whether my body was there or just my spirit, I don't know; only God knows. But I do know that I was caught up into paradise and heard things so astounding that they cannot be told."

Paul tells us in **PHILIPPIANS 1: 21-23** that he prefers to depart from the body and be with Christ in heaven. But because he wanted to preach the gospel he chose to stay in the body. Departing from the body means the spirit-man coming out of the body. Only the spirit can go to be with Christ when a man dies.

Paul boldly tells us also that he was cut up to third heaven in the paradise where God said so many things to him. His experience was similar to that of Prophet Ezekiel in that both occurred in the realm of the spirit but differs because Paul's spirit was caught up to heaven while Ezekiel spirit was taken to places in this world. In both cases the Holy Spirit was the initiator of the experience.

Paul was not dead when he was caught up; he came back to his body and taught the church of God so many mysteries. If not for Paul may be the church would have been ignorance of the spiritual warfare and our exalted position in Christ above all the powers of the devil. Thank God for his life! Some of the teachings of Paul were very hard to understand by the early Christians in his days. Many today still do not understand some of his teachings. Apostle

Peter pointed this out:

> 2 PETER 3:15, 16
> "Bear in mind that our Lord's patience means salvation, just as our dear **BROTHER PAUL ALSO WROTE TO YOU WITH THE WISDOM THAT THE LORD GAVE HIM.** He writes the same way in all his letters, speaking in them of these matters. **HIS LETTERS CONTAIN SOME THINGS THAT ARE HARD TO UNDERSTAND,** which ignorant and unstable people distort, as they do the other Scriptures, to their own destruction."

APOSTLE JOHN IN PATMOS & HEAVEN

John was physically banished to the island of Patmos because of his faith and testimony about Christ Jesus. It was in this island that God sent His angel from heaven to show him this glorious vision. From **REVELATION CHAPTER 1** to **CHAPTER 3**, God sent His angel to him in that island and opened his spiritual eyes to see this angel and the glorified Lord Jesus who spoke with him. At this level of vision John knew he was still in Patmos and was seeing a vision. He was commanded to write letters to seven churches in Asia Minor representing the churches of Christ in the entire world.

REVELATION 4: 1-3

"After these I looked, and there before me was a door standing open in heaven. And the voice I had first heard speaking to me like a trumpet said, 'COME UP HERE, and I will show you what must take place after this.' At once I was in the Spirit, and there before me was a throne in heaven with someone sitting on it."

The level of this vision changed when the Lord opened his eyes again to see the real heaven. One statement is worth taken note of here, *"And the voice... said... come up here..."* We must understand what happened here; the angel said he wanted to show him something but he was to *"come up here"*. Come up where? To the heaven of course! What happened after this? John said, *"At once I was in the Spirit, and there before me was a throne in heaven with someone sitting on it."*

The spirit-man left the material body on the island of Patmos and travelled to heaven to receive the message. It was so instant that John immediately found himself in heaven after the angel had said, *"come up here."* He was also caught up to heaven like Apostle Paul. This is very simple to understand.

These three great men of God experienced the *'spirit-man'* travelling in the spiritual realm – Ezekiel, Paul and John. Many other faithful children of God have had similar experiences and we know that it is true. We conclude that it is possible for the spirit-man to come out of the body to receive teachings and see many things in the spiritual realm.

But let us know that in the three examples sighted above, men were not the initiators of the experience but God himself who wanted to show His faithful servants the things He wanted them to know. The Lord may be willing to take anyone of us into this kind of spiritual experience there is no cause for alarm, we are His and are in His hand.

OCCULTISM

Exploring the spiritual realm is safe as long as it is by the Holy Spirit. Venturing to have spiritual experience outside the will of God is dangerous and occultic. Satan and his cohorts in the evil spiritual kingdom know this spiritual principle so well that he greatly employs it to enslave his captives, to give people false spiritual experience and to empower his mortal agents to perpetrate his evil activities in this world.

The experience of the spirit-man coming out of the material body while the body is not yet dead is called, *"Soul travels or Astral Projections"* in satanic kingdom and it can be done through some occultic methods like yoga or transcendal meditations and many others. We have heard of people with familiar spirits, witches and wizards, marine spirits, and other powerful occultic people travelling spiritually to the heavenlies, waters, and many other places to hold meetings and to meet with demons. All these people use this principle of *"soul travel"*. Through occultic means by demons their *"spirit-man"* is called out of the bodies into the spiritual realm. This takes place mainly while they sleep or during some yoga meditations.

Let us point out some of their devilish activities here, when some of these occultic people want to punish their victims, they will call out the spirit-man of the person to a shrine, river or anywhere they choose. They could pronounce curses on him, inflict injury on him, shoot him with a gun or stab with a knife, take things from him, put rags on him, even stripe him naked, have sexual intercourse with him or her or force him to agree to be initiated into occultism and so on.

Also, the occultic person could project his own spirit-man out to attack his victim. This usually happens when the victim is asleep, he may dream and see what happened or, they may blind his spiritual eyes so that he will not remember when he wakes up. Sooner or later, the victim will experience physically, the effect of the havoc done to him or her in the spiritual realm. This is called demonic manipulations; this sort is taking place everyday in this physical world. Through it Satan and all his cohorts are interfering seriously with our physical world.

In any case we Christians should not be afraid of all these things. Remember the word of God:

1 JOHN 5: 19, 20

"We know that we are children of God, and that the whole world is under the control of the evil one. We know also that the Son of God has come and has given us understanding, so that we may know him who is true. And we are in him who is true – even in his Son Jesus Christ. He is the true God and eternal life."

We have the understanding of the things of the spiritual realm because God through His Spirit in us has enlightened us. This is to make us rise up and destroy the works of the devil in the lives of the victims and our own lives as well because they try to manipulate us too. We must stand up and illuminate the people about the spiritual things, and to resist the devil and stop all his activities in our lives, families and others whom the Lord might lead us to help.

CHAPTER EIGHT

SATANIC INFLUENCE OVER THIS PRESENT WORLD |

The Lord Jesus Christ was fasting for forty days and nights in the wilderness in preparation for His earthly ministry. At the end, Satan showed up to tempt Him.

LUKE 4: 5, 6 KJV
"And the devil, taking him up into a high mountain, shewed unto him all the kingdoms of the world in a moment of time. And the devil said unto him, 'All this power will I give thee, and the glory of them: for that is delivered unto me; and to whomever I will I give it.'"

But, why should Satan come to tempt Jesus? All the hosts of evil kingdom heard the voice of God clearly during the baptism of Jesus Christ in river Jordan by John the Baptist saying *"This is my Beloved Son in whom I am well pleased."* They knew definitely that Jesus Christ was the Son of God, yet Satan came face to face to tempt Him. He wanted Jesus Christ to fall just like Adam and Eve in the garden. If Jesus falls, he would then take over Him and destroy the plan of redemption. Thank God that Jesus Christ overcame the devil's temptation.

Let us look critically at the statement of Satan in the text above, he led Jesus to a high place and showed Him all the kingdoms of the world and said, *"All this power will I give thee,... for that is delivered unto me"* (**VERSE 6**). Here Satan is boldly claiming his authority over the world and Jesus did not rebuke him for such a claim. Jesus knew he was saying the fact.

The big question is: Who delivered the kingdom of the world to Satan? Is it God? No. Bible shows us that God gave the kingdom of the world to human beings through Adam and Eve.

PSALM 115: 16
"The highest heavens belong to the LORD, but the earth he has given to man."

Satan was not happy about this, so he came to the garden, being a spirit and needed a physical body to attract Eve; he possessed the serpent so as to carry out his evil plan. Snake became the first animal to be possessed by the devil. That is why God cursed the snake and thereafter, Satan is referred to as the ancient serpent (**REVELATION 12: 9**). After the snake, Satan and his demons have been in the business of possessing both animal and human bodies and using them for evil activities.

He tempted Eve with food and she fell, through Eve he got Adam also. With this seemly simple act he stole the authority of the world from Adam. So, when Satan said to Jesus, *"It has been delivered unto me"* both Jesus and Satan knew that man delivered the world's authority to Satan. Right from the time men fell in the garden, the kingdom of the world has been spiritually controlled and dominated by the devil.

THE FORBIDDEN FRUIT

Man ate the fruit of knowledge of good and evil against God's will in the garden and became independent of God and consequently became the slave of Satan.

Amazingly, because the new ruler of mankind, that is Satan, is an evil spirit being, he accelerated the knowledge of evil in man and suppressed the knowledge of good. So in **GENESIS 4**, we see the first child of Adam filled with murderous thoughts and finally killed his brother, Abel.

In **GENESIS 6: 5-6**, (KJV) *"And God saw that the wickedness of man was great in the earth, and that every imagination of the thoughts of his heart was only evil continually. And it repented the LORD that he had made man on the earth, and it grieved him at his heart."* God regretted that He created man!

The mind and heart of man was the major target of the devil and he got it. The heart of man is like the steering that controls a car; whosoever holds it dictates the direction of that car. In the same way Satan polluted the mind of man. First, he snatched man's heart from God and man became spiritually dead to God, now he went further to corrupt the mind of man with evil desire and lust. The book of Romans relates to us the mind of a natural man.

ROMAN 1:28-31 KJV

"And even as they did not like to retain God in their knowledge, God gave them over to a reprobate mind, to do those things which are not convenient; Being filled with all unrighteousness, fornication, wickedness, covetousness, maliciousness, full of envy, murder, debate, deceit, malignity; whisperers, backbiters, haters of God, despiteful, proud, boasters, inventors of evil things, disobedient to parents, without understanding, covenant breakers, without natural affection, implacable, unmerciful:"

The man's mind is called *"a reprobate mind"* in the scripture above.

Corruptions and evils prevailing in our society today are enough evidence to show us that the influence of devil is over the people of this present age. Think about it, the system of this present age eradicated the knowledge of God from the public schools, virtually all the communication media: the internet, television and radio stations have been given to promote sexual immoralities; man to man now get married (homosexuality), woman to woman indulge in sexual act (lesbianism). Normal marriage between man and woman now becomes contract, and people are encouraged to divorce at will. The custom of single parenthood prevails in western world. People are no more ashamed of their wickedness.

In Europe, churches are virtually being closed down and alcoholic joints increases day by day. Wicked acts and crimes are alarmingly increasing all over the world. People both young and old are no more interested in the things of God. False religions spring up to mislead people. This indeed is a wicked and adulterous generation under the sway of demonic control. The devil and the hosts of hell try very hard up to this day to hinder the gospel of Christ from getting into the hearts of men. Apostle Paul reveals this to us in **2 CORINTHIANS 4: 4**. This shows why unbelievers do not have interest in the gospel. They are veiled!

Thank God for the Lord Jesus Christ who rescued us from the power of Satan and delivered us to the kingdom of God. (**COLOSSIANS.1: 13**). Through the Christians the Lord is delivering the people from the power of Satan. The presence of the church and the Holy Spirit resists the power of the devil greatly in this time.

SATANIC ADMINISTRATION

Let us get further understanding from the book of Daniel. In one of the visions shown to Daniel by God about the end time, he did not understand and thus determined to fast and pray to ask God for its meaning. He fasted for 21 days. But did God have to allow Daniel to fast and pray for such a long period before He answers him? Has He not said, *"Before they call I will answer; while they are speaking I will hear."* (ISAIAH 64: 2)?

Surprisingly on the 21st day, angel Gabriel came to him in a vision and said:

DANIEL 10: 12-13

"...Do not be afraid, Daniel. Since the first day that you set your mind to gain understanding and to humble yourself before your God, your words were heard, and I have come in response to them. But the prince of the Persian Kingdom resisted me twenty-one days. Then Michael, one of the chief princes, came to help me, because I was detained there with the king of Persia."

We see clearly from the scripture above that God gave answer to Daniel's prayer since the first day. He does not unnecessarily delay the answer to the prayers of His faithful children. But, who is this so called *"the prince of the Persian Kingdom"* who resisted the angel of the Lord for 21 days? Definitely it was not king Cyrus (DANIEL 10: 1), for he was a mortal man like Daniel and man cannot resist or detain angels.

"The prince of the Persian Kingdom" is the demonic prince, the beast, a spiritual member of the principalities and powers, the rulers of the darkness, the spiritual wickedness in the heavenly realm, which Apostle Paul talks about in **EPHESIANS 6:12**. Behind every physical governments of this world there is a spiritual counterpart. These evil spirit-rulers influence the physical government to take decisions, which is against God's word in this generation. That is one of the reason we, as Christians, are commanded in the scripture to always pray for the people in government. When we pray for them, we neutralise the influence of the devil over them.

We can now understand how Satan has gained control over the affair of the world's governments. Let me freely tell you brethren, there are satanic princes over the continents: Africa, Asia, America, Australia, and Europe. In every country for example, there is a demonic prince over its kingdom; each county, each province, each local areas has its own territorial demonic princes, which controls and influences it.

Satan is a *'good'* administrator, he has control over the world system, for example, he has succeeded in diverting the attention of the people from God to other things like sports especially football, the only sport that greatly harmonise the world. May God have mercy.

Angel Gabriel said to Daniel:

DANIEL 10: 20-21
"...Soon I will return to fight against the prince of Persia, and when I go, the prince of Greece will come;"

When he conquered the spiritual forces of the devil over Persian Empire, then the Greece Empire overthrew the physical government of Persia.

Brethren, Satan's evil government is the backbone of this present evil age; that is why evil is alarmingly and uncontrollably increasing. Christians must rise up to pray and destroy the plans of the devil over this world from time to time; this is our assignment on earth.

CHAPTER NINE

SPECIFIC SATANIC MANIPULATIONS I

2 CORINTHIANS 2:11
"In order that Satan might not outwit us. For we are not unaware of his schemes"

I want to endeavour in this chapter, to quickly scan through the scriptures and bring out some specific spiritual actions of the devil and his evil spirits over mankind and the corresponding manifestations in the physical realm. This is to make the children of God wise and be prepared to *"resist the devil and he will flee"* (James 4:7). Also to be able to discern his works in the lives of the victims so that those under his manipulations could be helped out.

I want you to know that Satan has not changed his strategy, he cannot hide before the search light of the Almighty God. All his works shall be exposed and destroyed in Jesus name. The Bible says:

HEBREWS 4: 13
"Nothing in all creation is hidden from God's sight. Everything is uncovered and laid bare

before the eyes of him to whom we must give account"

A. In The Garden Of Eden

God specifically told Adam, before the creation of Eve his wife, in the garden:

> **Genesis 2: 16, 17**
> "And the LORD God commanded the man, 'You are free to eat from any tree in the garden; but you must not eat from the tree of knowledge of good and evil, for when you eat of it you will surely die."

Adam told his wife about the commandments of God. Everything was going on well between them and God until the intruder, that evil teacher and counsellor showed up to tempt them. Satan came to Eve in the garden to tell her that God's word was a lie.

> **Genesis 3:4, 5**
> "You will not surely die,' the serpent said to the woman. 'For God knows that when you eat of it your eyes will be opened, and you will be like God, knowing good and evil."

Here is one of the secrets of Satan's work; he will always come to negate the truth of God's word. I told the youth in our church while studying the manipulations of the devil in the book of Genesis that, anyone in any manner who comes to them negating the word of God, they should discern that the devil himself is behind such acts. In the world presently many books are written, which are against God's word, many principles of life are laid down which is against God's ordinance. All these are spiritually inspired by the devil to go against God in this world.

He succeeded in destroying the harmonious relationship between Adam and God after he counselled them to eat from the forbidden fruit.

GENESIS 3: 8
"Then the man and his wife heard the sound of the LORD God as he was walking in the garden in the cool of the day, and they hid from the LORD God among the trees of the garden."

The voice of God their creator, which used to be pleasant to their hearing had now became dreadful to them. God became annoyed with them; He cursed the serpent and indirectly cursed Satan, too, who possessed the snake as an instrument. He cursed the woman also and cursed the land because of Adam (**GENESIS 3: 14-19**). At the end, God finally drove Adam and Eve out of the Garden of Eden (**GENESIS 4: 22, 23**).

Here shows plainly one of the works of the devil again; he will go to any extent to destroy a godly relationship. between man and God, husband and wife, and among the Christian fellowships. He hates people coming together to fellowship, praying or reading the word of God. If he is given the opportunity, he will sow seeds of discord so as to destroy such godly unions. Let us be careful and wise not to give audience to the devil when he comes to us in disguise.

Breakages and segregations in the church, fighting among church leaders and members and likes are the works of the devil. We should not entertain him as Eve did else he will use the one who is weak, careless and carnal who entertains him in his or her mind to destroy the things of God. Let it be known also that anyone who allows himself or herself to be used by the devil will also suffer divine punishment. Let us be admonished!

B. Manipulation Against Job

Job 1: 6-12

"One day the angels came to present themselves before the LORD, and Satan also came with them. The LORD said to Satan, 'Where have you come from?' Satan answered the LORD, 'From roaming through the earth and going to and fro in it.' Then the LORD said to Satan, 'Have you considered my servant Job? There is no-one on earth like him; he is blameless and upright, a man who fears God and shuns evil.' 'Does Job fear God for nothing?' Satan replied. 'Have you not put a hedge around him and his household and everything he has? You have blessed the works of his hands, so that his flocks and herds are spread throughout the land. But stretch out your hand and strike everything he has, and he will surely curse you to your face.' The LORD said to Satan, 'Very well, then, everything he has is in your hands, but on the man himself do not lay a finger.' Then Satan went out from the presence of the LORD"

The scripture above shows us that there are council meetings going on in the spiritual realm as well. All the heavenly hosts periodically present themselves before the Lord God their creator. In a similar manner the god of this present age, Satan the devil also holds his own conference with all his wicked hosts in the heavenly realm. Various meetings are going on from time to time in the realm of the spirit unknown to many people of this physical world. This truth is not a thing of the past but presently real in the realm of the spirit.

We see in the text above that Satan the accuser of brethren went to the highest heaven to present himself before the LORD in the midst of God's angels.

There is also another scene shown to us in the book of **1 King**:

1 KINGS 22: 19-22
"Micaiah continued, 'Therefore hear the word of the LORD: I saw the LORD sitting on his throne with all the host of heaven standing

round him on his right and on his left. And the LORD said, 'Who will entice Ahab into attacking Ramoth Gilead and going to his death there?' 'One suggested this, and another that. Finally, a spirit came forward, stood before the LORD and said, 'I will entice him.' 'By what means?' the LORD asked. 'I will go out and be a lying spirit in the mouth of all his prophets,' he said. 'You will succeed in enticing him,' said the LORD. 'Go and do it.'"

This was the vision shown to Prophet Micaiah. God had concluded that that wicked king of Israel, Ahab, must die because of his sins. Hear what the Bible records about him: *"There was never a man like Ahab, who sold himself to do evil in the eyes of the LORD, urged on by Jezebel his wife."* (1 KINGS 21:25). During one of the heavenly council meetings with God, an evil spirit from Satan showed up and said: *"I will go out and be a lying spirit in the mouth of his (Ahab's) prophets."* Presently in the world there are many so called prophets operating with lying spirits. Children of God must be warned lest they fall victims to them.

Whenever Satan or his evil angels presented themselves before the LORD in the Old Testament as we have seen, it is either to accuse the righteous or to be allowed to carry out certain destructive assignments.

We must see a clear difference between the spiritual and physical realm here; Satan said it plainly when asked by God where he came from: *"I have been going back and forth across the earth, watching everything that's going on."* (NLT). Can you see that? Satan and all his evil spirits are here with us in this planet earth watching and studying what we do.

Although we cannot see them, they are here carrying out their evil operations. No wonder God called this present age an *"evil age"* (GALATIANS 1:13).

Should Christians be afraid because Satan and all his hosts are present in this world? No! Let me tell us plainly from the word of Prophet Elisha: *"'Don't be afraid,' the prophet answered. 'Those who are with us are more than those who are with them.'"* (2 KINGS 6:16).

The hosts of heaven working for the children of God are far more and stronger than all the hosts of Satan combined. All the same, the Bible warns us to *"Be sober, be vigilant; because your adversary the devil, as a roaring lion, walketh about, seeking whom he may devour."* (1 PETER 5:8) KJV. We shall talk more about the authority of the believers over the devil in preceding chapters but it is very important for us to know what is happening around us. Ignorance is very dangerous!

Another important lesson to learn here is that discussions could be going on in the spiritual realm, decision could be taken and finalised without the physical realm knowing it. God and Satan were discussing about Job but Job being human, did not know. Finally the discussion was concluded: *"LORD said to Satan, 'Very well, then, everything he has is in your hands, but on the man himself do not lay a finger.' Then Satan went out from the presence of the LORD."* (VERSE 12).

When I personally learnt this secret, I have since not stopped to cry out in the place of prayer, saying: *"Any evil conversations, or any evil committee set up to discuss against me, my home, job or ministry in the realm of the spirit or the physical, be shattered by Holy Ghost fire in Jesus name"*. We should not be ignorant of the fact that before some things happen physically they had been concluded spiritually.

Satan left the presence of God to call another meeting of his own evil spirits and planned how to attack Job. The physical manifestations of satanic actions against Job are recorded:

JOB 1: 13-19

"One day when Job's sons and daughters were feasting and drinking wine at the oldest brother's house, a messenger came to Job and said, 'The oxen were ploughing and the donkeys were grazing nearby, and the Sabeans attacked and carried them off. They put the servants to the sword, and I am the only one who has escaped to tell you!'...another messenger came and said, 'The fire of God fell from the sky and burned up the sheep and the servants, and I am the only one who has escaped to tell you!'...another messenger came and said, 'The Chaldeans formed three raiding parties and swept down on your camels and carried them off. They put the servants to the sword, and I am the only one who escaped to tell you!'... yet another messenger came and said, 'Your sons and daughters were feasting and drinking wine at the oldest brother's house, when suddenly a mighty wind swept in from the desert and struck the four corners of the house. It collapsed on them and they are dead, I am the only one who has escaped to tell you!'"

I want us to briefly consider the physical disasters, which befell Job in the account above. First, *"the Sabeans,"* the group of raiders attacked his servants, put them to sword, and made away with Job's donkeys. The third disaster is similar to the first one, *"The Chaldeans formed three raiding parties and swept down on your (Job's) camels and carried them off. They put the servants to the sword..."*

In these set of two disasters, Satan inspired men to attack Job's properties. We must understand here what the devil is capable of doing; he can put thoughts in peoples' mind and inspire them to carry it out. A carnal reasoning may say that the attack of the Sabeans and the Chaldeans were just natural, well, that is the way men reason, but thank God for the scriptures which reveals to us the evil spiritual forces that were behind it. These Sabeans and Chaldeans raiders had been existing yet couldn't think of attacking Job because the Bible says, God had put a hedge all around him and his family and properties – this is a spiritual hedge and not a physical one. We must all understand this. After Satan had taken permission to attack Job then he employed the instrumentality of men to come against his properties.

One thing worth noticing also is that those people used against Job might not even be aware that satanic forces from the spirit realm were inspiring them, they might have though that it was by their own actions. But God's Word tells us that these people were under satanic influence and were led to Job's direction. In the New testament Ananias and Sapphira never knew that Satan was behind their evil thought and discussions to lie to the minister of God until the man of God confronted them, saying, *"HOW IS IT THAT SATAN HAS SO FILLED YOUR HEART THAT YOU HAVE LIED TO THE HOLY SPIRIT and have kept for yourself some of the money you received from the land..."* (ACTS 5: 1-11).

Up till now we must know that so many people are under the influence of the devils in certain actions they undertake knowingly and unknowingly to them. We must also understand that wars among nations can and are mainly caused by satanic influences on the people. Spiritually sensitive people will discern this.

Considering the second and the forth disaster which Satan brought upon Job, we can see also here that Satan does not only have the power to influence the thoughts and actions of men, but he could also command fire from the sky to *"burn up the sheep and the servants." He could command "a mighty wind swept in from the desert and struck the four corners of the house"* to collapse the house on Job's children and kill them. We see in EXODUS 5:8-13 that he could perform miracles also: Moses' rod turned to snake by the power of God, the magicians – Satan's human servants, also dropped their own sticks and they became snakes, but the snake of God swallowed up the magicians' snake. Thank God for the supremacy of His power over the devil.

Many occurrences in this our world, which people termed as ordinary and natural disasters could be as a result of the finished works in the spirit realm.

Honestly, we people of this world don't know the magnitude of the spiritual forces that are influencing our physical world and us. The people of this physical world run around and groan when calamity befalls them but most of the time the source is from the spirit realm. Thank God who has given us this spiritual understanding. We should not be lazy in prayer to nullify the operations and influences of Satan against us as individuals, our family, community, country and the whole world at large. Remember God warns us in the book of **REVELATION**:

REVELATION 12: 12
"But woe to the earth and the sea, because the devil has gone down to you! He is filled with fury, because he knows that his time is short."

Satan planed his attack against Job so that Job could curse God. That was his aim and objective – to make Job curse God! Satan succeeded in destroying every property of Job including his children. But the Bible says, *"In all this, Job did not sin by charging God with wrongdoing"* (**VERSE** 22). Unlike many people today Christians inclusive, when in difficulties or certain bad situations, the first thing they do is to pass insults on God. They do this because of their lack of knowledge. Everybody should learn from this.

I thought Satan would hands up here, but no! He went again to God during another council meeting of heaven to accuse Job and seek permission to afflict him with sickness.

JOB 2: 6-8
"The Lord said to Satan, 'very well, then, he is in your hand; but you must spare his life.' So Satan went out from the presence of the LORD and afflicted Job with painful sores from the soles of his feet to the top of his head. Then Job

took a piece of broken pottery and scraped himself with it as he sat among the ashes."

Satan is very wicked. He has indeed come to steal, to kill and to destroy. He and his angels are well described by Apostle Paul as *"the spiritual wickedness in the heavenly realm."*

Thanks to the Lord although it was a tough time for Job, in the end God restored him:

JOB 42: 12, 16, 17
"The LORD blessed the latter part of Job's life more than the first... After this, Job lived a hundred and forty years; he saw his children and their children to the fourth generation. And he died, old and full of years."

CLARIFICATION

JOB 2: 6
"The Lord said to Satan, 'very well, then, he is in your hand; but you must spare his life."

We can also notice in the scripture above that Satan could kill human beings. Had God not warned him against Job's life he could decide to kill him.

Are the Christians now at the mercy of Satan? Shall we fear him? Does he have power over us? Well, we should not be confused about this, that in the Old Testament he had power over all humans because Adam sold the human race out to him. The

Lord Jesus had not come to the world to die then, so according to the spiritual principle, Satan could be feared in the Old Testament. But now all things have changed; Jesus came to the world, conquered Satan and delivered us from sin and his grip:

COLOSSIANS 1:13
"For he has rescued us from the dominion of darkness and brought us into the kingdom of the Son he loves, in whom we have redemption, the forgiveness of sins."

HEBREWS 2: 14
"Since the children have flesh and blood, he (Jesus) too share in their humanity so that by his death he might destroy him who holds the power of death – that is, the devil – and free those who all their lives were held in slavery by their fear of death."

Before the Lord Jesus ascended to heaven, He said about the Christians:

LUKE 10: 19
"I have given you authority to trample on the snakes and scorpions and to overcome all the power of the enemy; nothing will harm you."

Apostle John tells us:

1 JOHN 4: 4
"You, dear children, are from God and have overcome them, because the one who is in you is greater than the one who is in the world."

In every spiritual right all Christians are greater than the devil and his evil spirits. (More of this in chapter ten).

Satan cannot go to the highest heaven anymore to accuse us before God; he has been cast out.

REVELATION. 12: 7-9

"And there was war in heaven. Michael and his angels fought against the dragon, and the dragon and his angels fought back. But he was not strong enough, and they lost their place in heaven. The great dragon was hurled down-that ancient serpent called the devil, or Satan, who leads the whole world astray. He was hurled to the earth, and his angels with him."

The Lord Jesus is seated enthroned in heaven now. Satan cannot show up in heaven anymore. Hallelujah! So brethren I tell you, do not be afraid of Satan, you are greater than him now, you are not at his mercy, and he has no power over you. We as God's children have absolute power and authority over him.

ADMONITION

JAMES 4: 7

"Submit yourselves, then, to God. Resist the devil, and he will flee from you."

We must not be spiritually ignorant but should submit to the spiritual laws of God so that Satan will not take advantage of us. We must not be disobedient to God.

> **EPHESIANS 2: 2 KJV**
> "Wherein in time past ye walked according to the course of this world, according to the prince of the power of the air, the spirit that now worketh in the children of disobedience:"

Any disobedience can give Satan the chance to work against the Christians. Let us be careful and lean on God's grace.

C. SPIRIT OF RIGHTEOUS MAN CALLED FROM THE DEAD

There is a scenario we need to pay great attention to in **1 SAMUEL CHAPTER 28**. God had rejected Saul the first king of Israel. Prophet Samuel had died and buried in Ramah, his hometown. While Saul was still on the Lord's side, he had expelled the mediums and spiritists (witches, wizards and those who had familiar spirits) from the land. This was in accordance with God's instruction in the book of **DEUTERONOMY**:

> **DEUTERONOMY 18: 10-13**
> "Let no-one be found among you who sacrifices his son or daughter in the fire, who practises divination or sorcery, interprets omens, engages in witchcraft, or cast spells, or who is a medium or spiritist or who consults the dead. Anyone

who does these things is detestable to the LORD, and because of these detestable practices the LORD your God will drive out those nations before you. You must be blameless before the LORD your God."

Then at a certain time there was a war between Israel and Philistine. When Saul saw the army of the enemy he became afraid and tried to consult the Lord for guidance on how to win the war but *"the Lord did not answer him by dreams or Urim or prophets"* (**VERSE 26**). Why? Because he had turned against the Lord in disobedience.

Finally, Saul fell back to a woman who used familiar spirits and asked her to bring up the spiritman of Prophet Samuel from the dead so that he could inquire from him what to do to win the war.

1 SAMUEL 28: 8-14

"So Saul disguised himself...and at night he and two men went to the woman. "Consult a spirit for me" he said "and bring up for me the one I name"...Then the woman asked, " Whom shall I bring up for you?" "Bring up Samuel," he said... The king said to her, "Don't be afraid. What do you see?" The woman said, "I see a spirit coming up out of the ground." "What does he look like?" he asked. "An old man wearing a robe is coming up," she said. Then Saul knew it was Samuel, and bow down and prostrated himself with his face to the ground."

The summary of what happened here is that, through a demonic conjurer the spirit-man of a righteous prophet was summoned from the dead.

This issue was once debated seriously some years back in our school fellowship during the Bible study section. We were all at the growing stage then. The main question here is: How could an occultist summon the spirit of a righteous man? Some said it was not the real Samuel that was brought up because, according to them, it was impossible for Satan to touch the righteous, so it must have been a demon in disguise. Others said it was Samuel. Many of us were confused about how to explain or interpret the passage, so we decided to leave it until later. As I grow in spiritual understanding the whole issue became clearer to me.

Surely the spirit of the person summoned was Samuel's. Bible makes it clear in VERSE 15-19:

1 SAMUEL 28: 15-19

"Samuel said to Saul, 'Why have you disturbed me by bringing me up?' 'I am in great distress,' Saul said. 'The Philistines are fighting against me, and God has turned away from me. He no longer answers me, either by prophets or by dreams. So I have called on you to tell me what to do.' Samuel said, 'Why do you consult me, now that the LORD has turned away from you and become your enemy? The LORD has done what he predicted through me. The LORD has torn the kingdom out of your hands and given it to one of your neighbours – to David. Because you did not obey the LORD or carry out his fierce wrath against the Amalekites, the LORD has done this to you today. The LORD will hand over both Israel and you to the Philistines, and tomorrow you and your sons will be with me. The LORD will also hand over the army of Israel to the Philistines. Immediately Saul fell full length on the ground, filled with fear because of Samuel's words..."

Samuel and Saul really discussed here as we have read.

Now this can not happen again. Do not misquote me, I am not saying that occultic powers could not call out the spirit of the dead anymore, in fact they still do. What I am saying is that the spirit of any righteous person, a saint in Christ, who has died, cannot be summoned by the devils anymore. *Why?* You may ask. First, Satan has no power over the Christians in the New Testament. Secondly, whenever a true child of God dies the spirit-man goes to heaven to be with Christ.

When Stephen was about to die in ACTS CHAPTER 7:

ACTS 7:56 - 60

"'Look,' he (Stephen) said, 'I see heaven open and the Son of Man standing at the right hand of God.'... While they were stoning him,

Stephen prayed, 'Lord Jesus, receive my spirit.' Then he fell on his knees and cried out, 'Lord, do not hold this sin against them.' When he had said this, he fell asleep."

Let all Christians be sure of this. Although Satan can still disguise as an angel of light yet he can no longer deceive us. We have the understanding through the Holy Spirit.

D. FILTHY GARMENT ON THE SPIRITMAN OF THE PRIEST OF GOD

ZECHARIAH 3: 1-5

"Then he showed me Joshua the high priest standing before the angel of the LORD, and Satan standing at his right side to accuse him. The LORD said to Satan, 'The LORD rebuke you Satan! The LORD, who has chosen Jerusalem, rebuke you! Is not this man a burning stick snatched from fire?' Now Joshua was dressed in filthy clothes as he stood before the angel. The angel said to those who were standing before him, 'Take off his filthy clothes.' Then he said to Joshua, 'See, I have taken away your sin, and I will put rich garments on you.' Then I said, 'Put a clean turban on his head.' So they put a clean turban on his head and clothed him, while the angel of the LORD stood by."

God opened the spiritual eyes of Prophet Zechariah so that he could see into the spirit realm. The angel of the Lord was sent to him to reveal some things about the nation of Israel. One of the things revealed was the spiritual condition of Joshua the High Priest. Priest Joshua was standing before the angel and Satan stood at his right side to accuse him. Not only that, he was dressed in filthy clothes as he stood before the angel.

In the physical realm, the High Priest in Israel would normally wear a gorgeous priestly garment as described in **EXODUS CHAPTER 39**. This garment was on Joshua in the physical realm but a filthy garment was on him when viewed in the spiritual realm. In the physical realm he was probably standing before mortal men but in the spiritual realm we see him standing before the angel of God, and Satan at his right side. This may sound impossible to some people, but to those who have the understanding of spiritual things it is not a puzzle at all.

What does it mean for Satan to stand at the right side of the man of God? Right side means the position of authority; the Lord Jesus Christ is now seated at God's right hand in heaven where He rules over all things in heaven and on earth.

Satan had usurped the spiritual authority of Joshua the High Priest; although he was still the high priest in the physical, he had no spiritual authority. This reveals the situation of many ministers of God in this generation. Yes, people know them as Apostles, Prophets, Pastors, Teachers or Evangelists but alas, they have lost their spiritual authority before God. Satan has gained entrance into their lives through carelessness and sins to rob them of their authority. They are thus empty and ordinary sounding cymbals.

These kinds of people struggle much in the ministry without tangible results. Some of them result in worldly charisma to get people into exciting emotional state making them to believe that the Holy Spirit is working among them yet the fruit of the Spirit, which characterised the growing Christian is absent in their lives. Some further resort into seeking the devil for demonic powers to do the work of God. They perform all kinds of false miracles to mislead the people. Christ is coming soon to judge the secret of men's heart!

The spirit-man of Joshua the high priest was clothed with filthy garment. Many people today are also walking about with clothes in the physical realm while actually, when viewed in the spiritual light of God, they are in rags or worst still, naked. This is one of the ways Satan tampers with peoples' lives in the realm of the spirit. The one that wears rags or is naked in the spiritual realm can never achieve anything good in the physical realm.

RESTORATION

At the heavenly command, Satan was rebuked, the filthy garment was taken off, and the new spiritual garment was put on him. The Lord then warned him to walk uprightly before Him.

This man's life was corrected spiritually before he achieved any success in the physical. There are so many manipulations of the devils against the 'spiritman' of people in this world, that is the reason evils and problems abound everywhere. This world's problem is not first of all a physical one; it is a spiritual one. We are only seeing the manifestations of what has been done in the spiritual realm. Only the Lord Jesus can solve the problem of people in this world.

When I became a Christian, I cried to God in prayers several times that I must not walk in spiritual blackout. I knew certainly that there were manipulations of the devil against my life because of the occultic foundations in my earthly family lineage. I always cried to God to show me my spiritual conditions so that I could know how to pray aright. The Lord in His mercy granted my desires.

Let me just mention few of the revelations I saw about myself on different occasions during and after prayers: I saw myself being naked; I saw myself wearing rags; I saw myself walking without a head,

I saw myself covered with something like a very big cotton wool in my mouth so that I could not talk and many more. Each of these revelations led me into serious prayers.

Now I thank the Lord for, *"many are the affliction of the righteous but the Lord delivers him from them all"* (**PSALM 34:19**). I am now praying the prayer of Apostle Paul in **EPHESIANS**, *"I pray that out of his glorious riches he may strengthen you with power through his Spirit in your inner being"* (**EPHESIANS 3:16**).

I always cry, *"Oh Lord let my spirit-man be strengthened against all satanic manipulations in the spiritual realm."* I am also heeding the admonition of Apostle Peter, *"Be sober, be vigilant; because your adversary the devil, as a roaring lion, walketh about, seeking whom he may devour"* (1 **PETER** 5: 8) KJV.

Brethren, God is on our side. Satan has no right to treat us as he does the people of world who have not given their lives to Christ.

CHAPTER TEN

THE HEIRS OF GOD'S KINGDOM

ROMAN 8:16, 17
"The Spirit himself testifies with our own spirit that we are God's children. Now if we are children, then we are heirs – heirs of God and co-heirs with Christ, if indeed we share in his sufferings in order that we may also share in his glory"

1 JOHN 3:1
"How great is the love the Father has lavished on us, that we should be called children of God! And that is what we are!..."

The greatest discovery I have made in life is to know truly that I am a child of this glorious Eternal Spirit-God who created all things for Himself. I am so happy to know that really I am one of the heirs, joint-heirs with Christ Jesus. It sounds so amazing to know this mysterious truth.

THE LORD JESUS CHRIST-THE HEIR

HEBREWS 1: 3
"The Son is the radiance of God's glory and the exact representation of his being..."

COLOSSIANS 1: 15-19
"He is the image of the invisible God, the firstborn over all creation. For by him all things were created: things in heaven and on earth, visible and invisible, whether thrones or power or rulers or authorities; all things were created by him and for him.... For God was pleased to have all his fullness dwell in him."

God's word says the Lord Jesus Christ is the exact radiant image of the invisible God and that God is pleased to have His fullness dwell in Him. Every authority in heaven and on earth belongs to Him. He is indeed the Heir of God.

Everything that is God's belongs to Christ Jesus. When He was about to ascend to heaven He said to the whole world, *"... All authority in heaven and on earth has been given to me."* (MATTHEW 28: 18).

God has willed every of his assets to Him because He is the Heir of His Kingdom. In the book of Revelation we see clearly that Christ Jesus sits on the throne at the right hand of God – the place of authority. All the hosts of heaven and the earth honour and worship Christ Jesus as they do to God Himself. Jesus Christ is indeed the Heir of God's kingdom!

> REVELATION 5: 14
> "Then I heard every creature in heaven and on earth and under the and on the sea, and all that is in them, singing: 'To him who sits on the throne and to the Lamb (Christ Jesus) be praise and honour and glory and power, for ever and ever!'"

WE ARE JOINT-HEIRS WITH CHRIST

God's Word says we are joint-heirs with His only begotten Son. After His resurrection, Christ is no more called *"the only begotten Son"* but *"the first begotten Son"* of the father because we have become His brethren as we become born again. God placed us in Christ having removed us from Adam. In Christ all authority in heaven and on earth also belong to us.

Every task accomplished by Jesus on earth was done because of us. He shed His blood and died to wipe away our sins and to put an end to the adamic nature, the old man, in us. He resurrected to give us a new life and a new beginning. He ascended and now sits on the throne to show us that indeed all authority in heaven and on earth belongs to Him. When He ascended to heaven He sent the Holy

Spirit to empower us in this world proving that we are the children of God. God thus declares us to be joint-heirs with His Son. Everything that belongs to God belongs to Christ and everything that belongs to Christ belongs to us – Halleluah!

As Christ sits on the throne in heaven, God's Word says we are seated with Him spiritually:

EPHESIANS 2: 6
"And God raised us with Christ and seated us with him in the heavenly realms in Christ Jesus…"

We are indeed joint-heir with the Lord Jesus Christ; His position is also our position. Glory to God who made it so!

BORN INTO THE KINGDOM

You cannot become the member of God's Kingdom unless you are born into it. The Lord said to Nicodemus, one of Israel's rulers:

JOHN 3: 3
"In reply Jesus declared, 'I tell you the truth, no one can see the kingdom of God unless he is born again.'"

Anyone who wants to be a joint-heir of God's Kingdom must believe in the finished work of salvation wrought by the Lord Jesus. He shed His blood as the Lamb of God, who takes away the sins of the whole world (**JOHN 1:29**).

How then do I become born-again? Simple! I must believe that Jesus died for my sins and then ask Him to forgive my sins.

1 JOHN 1:8, 9
"If we claim we to be without sin, we deceive ourselves and the truth is not in us. If we confess our sins, he is faithful and just and will forgive us our sins and purify us from all unrighteousness."

I must confess Him as my Lord and personal saviour:

ROMANS 10: 9
"That if you confess with your mouth, 'Jesus is Lord,' and believe in your heart that God raised him from the dead, you will be saved."

As I do this in faith, instantly God accepts me and sends His Spirit into my heart (**ROMANS 8:15, 16**). Then with thanksgiving I rise up as a born-again child of God. By God's grace I now make a commitment to serve Him all my life. The Holy Spirit is within me to lead me in the way of the Lord and to create the eagerness in me to grow in the knowledge of God's Word (**ROMANS 6: 23; 1 PETER 2: 2,3**).

If you are not yet a member of God's Kingdom, sincerely follow the step above, the hosts of heaven will welcome you and your name will be written into the book of life in heaven.

LUKE 15: 10
"In the same way, I tell you, there is rejoicing in the presence of the angels of God over one sinner who repents."

The Lord Jesus said to His disciples and to us, *"... rejoice that your names are written in heaven."* (LUKE 10: 20).

THE FAMILY OF GOD'S KINGDOM

Whenever anyone is born-again certain things happen to him or her spiritually: first, he is taken away from Adam into Christ. That is, his ancestry is no more in Adam but in Christ. We must understand that the authority of Satan reigns in Adam. A born again child of God is dead with Christ on the cross to sin and adamic nature, the old man, hence he is no more under the authority of Satan but instead he belongs to the Kingdom of God. That is why **COLOSSIANS 1: 13** makes it very clear to us:

COLOSSIANS 1:13
"For he has rescued us from the dominion of darkness and brought us into the kingdom of the Son he loves, in whom we have redemption, the forgiveness of sins."

HEBREWS CHAPTER 12 shows us the group we belong to as we become born-again:

HEBREWS 12: 22-24
"But you have come to Mount Zion, to the heavenly Jerusalem, the city of the living God. You have come to thousands upon thousands of angels in joyful assembly, to the church of the firstborn, whose names are written in heaven. You have come to God, the judge of all men, to the spirits of righteous men made perfect, to Jesus the mediator of a new covenant, and to the sprinkled blood that speaks a better word than the blood of Abel."

We belong to heaven where God dwells. We belong to the companies of the heavenly angels; these angels serve us as heirs of salvation.

HEBREWS 1: 14
"Are not all angels ministering spirits sent to serve those who will inherit salvation?"

We have come to be members of Christ's church and our names are written in heaven. We belong to the company of the righteous men of old, which we read about in the scripture: Abraham, Enoch, Abel, Moses, Elijah, David, Daniel, Solomon etc. Above all, we belong to the Lord Jesus Christ the mediator of the New Testament.

Each time Satan tries to embarrass me, I just rise up and command him to be quiet because I know the son of whom I am and where I belong. He or his demons has no right over my life because I am not in his kingdom. I am in the Kingdom of God's dear Son as His joint-heir.

I AM NOT ALONE

Because I belong to Christ, I know that I am not alone; The Holy Spirit dwells in me, the angels and all heavenly hosts are all around me. They are ready to serve me and fight my battles. Although I don't see them physically, but by faith I know they are with me.

The book of **2 KINGS CHAPTER 6** is a good illustration to show you this. Prophet Elisha, the man of God woke up one morning only to discover that the army of the enemy of Israel had surrounded the city where he was, and ready to arrest him:

2 KINGS 6: 15-17

"When the servant of the man of God got up and went out early the next morning, an army with horses and chariots had surrounded the city. 'Oh, my lord, what shall we do?' the servant asked. 'Don't be afraid,' the prophet answered. 'Those who are with us are more than those who are with them.' And Elisha prayed, 'O LORD, open his eyes so that he may see.' Then the LORD opened the servant's eyes, and he looked and saw the hills full of horses and chariots of fire all round Elisha."

The spiritual eye of the servant of the man of God was opened and he saw in reality that they were not alone there. The heavenly hosts were with them and were far more than the enemy. Brethren, just believe this, heavenly hosts are with all God's children to fight their battles. **PSALM 34: 7** assures us that, *"The angel of the LORD encamps around those who fear him, and delivers them."* In a similar manner God's Word also tells us that:

1 JOHN 4: 4
"You, dear children, are from God and have overcome them, because the one who is in you is greater than the one who is in the world."

He that is in us is the Lord Jesus Christ in the person of the Holy Spirit. He is the same one who sits enthroned in heaven filling the whole universe. He that is in the world is the god of this present evil age, the defeated Satan and his cohorts. I know the truth; I am not alone because God dwells in me and the hosts of heaven are all around me. I am greater than the devil and his entire hosts put together.

Satan does not want us to know this truth because the revelation knowledge of it will devastate his kingdom. So he tries hard to make sure that Christians are ignorant of their position and authority in Christ. But now the veil of ignorance is torn to pieces. We are rising to silence every manipulations of the devil in this generation in Jesus name.

GROW IN ALL SPIRITUAL UNDERSTANDING

COLOSSIANS 1: 9,10
"For this reason, since we the day we heard about you, we have not stopped praying for you and asking God to fill you with the knowledge of his will through all spiritual wisdom and understanding"

1 CORINTHIANS 2: 12
"We have not received the spirit of the world but the Spirit who is from God, that we may understand what God has freely given us."

As God's children, we are called to grow in spiritual understanding. We must know what happens in the physical realm as well as the spiritual. We must be spiritually sensitive. We are called to fight the unseen battle therefore spiritual understanding is inevitable for our victory (**EPHESIANS 6: 12**).

Satanic veil must not cover our minds. We must be able to discern things going around us so that Satan will not take advantage of us. Bible states clearly that ignorance is dangerous.

HOSEA 4: 6
"my people are destroyed from lack of knowledge."

What the scientists cannot explain, we are given

the spiritual insight to explain. Every counterfeit spirituality of the devil must be discerned and exposed. The light of God's truth must shine through us for the world to see. Thus Apostle Paul prayed certain prayers for Ephesians' Christians and urged us to pray these prayers also:

EPHESIANS 1: 17-21

"I keep asking that the God of our Lord Jesus Christ, the glorious Father, may give you the spirit of wisdom and revelation, so that you may know him better. I pray also that the eyes of your heart may be enlightened in order that you may know the hope to which he has called you, the riches his glorious inheritance in the saints, and his incomparable great power for us who believe. That power is like the working of his mighty strength, which he exerted in Christ when he raised him from the dead and seated him at his right hand in the heavenly realm, far above all rule and authority, power and dominion, and every title that can be given, not only in the present age but also in the one to come."

We need to know God better. Knowing God means learning more of His ways: how does He do His things? What has He said about Himself? What are His wills as revealed in His Word? How strong is He? What did He say about human beings and Christians, those in Christ? What did He say about the devil and his ways? What did He say about the future of all things? And so on. These and more are what we still need to know about God. We cannot learn these with our natural wisdom because God is Spirit. The Bible says:

1 CORINTHIANS 2: 14
"The man without the Spirit does not accept the things that come from the Spirit of God, for they are foolishness to him, and he cannot understand them, because they are spiritually discerned."

That is why the first condition to be met in knowing God is to be born-again. A born-again person becomes a child of God because he has the life of God in him through the Holy Spirit. Apostle Paul says it is imperative for us to grow in the knowledge of God. We must therefore pray for the spirit of wisdom and revelation. In VERSE 18 above, he says we should pray for our eyes of understanding to be enlightened. I call this divine illumination. This makes those who have it gain great insight into the things of the Spirit of God.

We need to know *"the hope to which he has called (us)..."* that is, the hope we have in God as He called us into His Kingdom, *"and what is the riches of the glory of his inheritance in the saints"*. Paul is enlightening us here that our inheritance in Christ is glorious and rich; we have to pray for revelation understanding to know the depth of the riches of our calling in Christ Jesus. May God give us understanding.

Apostle Paul goes further to describe the power of God, which is working for us and in us as Christians; God has channelled His power to work on our behalf in this present world. Note the description of that power which is available for us as God's children in Christ; it is called *"the incomparably great power"* in **NIV** and *"the exceeding greatness of his power"* in **KJV**. Paul began to describe the effectiveness of this power: it is the power that raised Christ from death; it is the power that enabled Him to ascend and no forces of evil in heavenly realm and on earth could pull Him down; it is the power that enthroned Him in the right hand of God.

In EPHESIANS 2:10 we read that, ***"And God raised us up with Christ and seated us with him in the heavenly realms in Christ Jesus."***

We must see that the position where the power of God exalts the Lord Jesus to is where we are as an individual Christian and as the church at large. This means that this great power of God in us is *"far above all principalities and powers..."* Thank God for this glorious inheritance we have as Christians, the body of Christ. It trills me to know that I am far greater than all the forces of the devils combined!

There are so many mysteries, which were not revealed to the Old Testament prophets, but now in

Christ Jesus, God has chosen to reveal them to us (**EPHESIANS 3: 2-6,9,10**).

God has determined to humiliate the devil in this generation, and has predetermined to use us, the Church, to show His manifold wisdom to principalities and powers in the heavenly realm (**EPHESIANS 3: 10**). Therefore, every secret of the devil must be uncovered. The church must manifest to destroy evil works in this present age. We must rise up to enlighten the people of this world and to tear down every veil, which Satan has used to cover their minds.

As we pray and get understanding from the Word of God through the Holy Spirit, the task given to us by God will become easily accomplished. Glory to God.

CHAPTER ELEVEN

CALLED TO DOUBLE UNDERSTANDING |

Christians are called to have double understanding, to see things from two perspectives. We are to view things in this world from both spiritual and physical perspectives. We are sent by the Eternal Spirit-God, to open the eyes of the spiritually blind people so that they may see and turn to God for their salvation.

Thank God for giving us the Bible, the most marvellous book in the whole world! It is a special package from God given to His children in order to reveal tremendous insights to us. Out of the Bible comes double revelation about anything we read from it. It gives us both spiritual and physical revelations.

Let us show some examples:

ONE

In the book of **GENESIS CHAPTER 1**; it reveals the Spirit-God who lives eternally, creating the physical world. This Invisible God calling unto others in the spirit realm saying *"Let us make man in our own image, in our own likeness ..."* It shows the invisible hand of God moulding physical clay into a certain shape – the shape of the Invisible God Himself.

The first people created, Adam and Eve, knew exactly that they had a creator who is Spirit, they related with Him, and they also relate with the physical world around them. So Adam and Eve had double understanding – the spiritual and as well as the physical.

We Christians are also human, and we have general understanding of our physical world just like all other people, but God called us out of the world to understand all things from the spiritual perspective also.

We see clearly in the book of **EPHESIANS 6** that we are called to fight a spiritual battle; to war against evil spiritual hosts causing problems and calamities in this physical world. I have said it earlier that the problems of this world are not originally physical but spiritual, but canal people will not see it this way. We Christians have the understanding. God who called us to fight against these spiritual hosts has given us His Spirit so that we can see and understand the things of the spiritual realm, and most importantly He has given us the Bible, His written Word, full of both spiritual and physical explanations of all things, so that we can be well informed.

Two

Looking at the book of **DANIEL CHAPTER 10**, we see Daniel fasting and praying for twenty-one days. If you were there, you could have easily asked, *"Daniel what are you doing?"* and he would have replied, *"I am fasting and praying."* The Bible gives us this physical information about Daniel here.

But it went further to give us the spiritual information also; we see what was going on in the realm of the spirit as Daniel was praying physically. God had sent His angel, Gabriel by name, down from heaven to give answer to Daniel's prayer but at the spiritual entrance into that country, another evil angel from Satan called ***"the prince of the Persian kingdom"*** had detained the angel sent by God so that he could not enter into the country.

Please let us get the understanding of things here, in the physical realm every nation has its own entrance, and immigration officers are put to guard the entrance into the nations. Supposing you're going into a particular nation to visit your friend, and at the airport the immigration officers stop you, queries you and found certain items, which they feel, should not come into their country, they can detain you or send you back to where you're coming from. We all understand this.

This is similar in the spiritual realm. Daniel was in a country called Persia and a visitor from another spiritual country called *"heaven"* was coming to deliver a message to him, but at the spiritual entrance of that nation the spiritual custom officer, an evil angel of Satan called **"*the prince of the Persian kingdom*"** detained him because he did not want the message of God to get to Daniel. What a revelation!

We Christians have the understanding that every nation has its own spiritual-entrance as well as the physical ones, spirit-rulers as well as the physical ones etc. We know what is called *"the satanic territorial spiritual administration"* over this world. We can easily discern the spiritual influences of the devil and his evil spirit beings over a nation, state, community, family, and an individual. We know how to pull down the strong hold of the devil anywhere we discern his works. We know how to battle the authority of the devil in the realm of the spirit and obtain victory, so that we can have our ways in the physical realm. We understand why evangelism is hard in certain nations and areas; we know that the territorial spirit-rulers of satanic kingdom are at work. We know how to conquer them and have our ways to win souls.

THREE

Let me give you one more example, I challenge you to read more from God's Word. In **MATTHEW CHAPTER 28**:

MATTHEW 28: 2
"There was a violent earthquake, for an angel of the Lord came down from heaven and, going to the tomb, rolled back the stone and sat on it."

The first information here is that the physical stone was been rolled away. A natural man may wonder what could have rolled away the stone since no human being touched it? But thank God the Word of God further tells us what had happened in the spiritual realm – the physical stone was rolled away by an angel in the realm of the spirit.

I can continue to give you numerous examples. The point, which the Holy Spirit wants us to know, is that the Lord has called us to understand and view issues from double perspectives; to see what is happening spiritually and the corresponding manifestations in the physical. As a Christian, each time I open my Bible to explore, with the inner Teacher and Counsellor – the Holy Spirit within me, mysteries are revealed, insights are given and understanding is achieved. Thank God for His glorious calling upon His people. What the scientists can't explain, we have been sent by God to give them the understanding. We are sent to open the eyes of the spiritually blind!

THE SPIRITUAL MAN JUDGES ALL THINGS

1 CORINTHIANS 2: 15
"The spiritual man makes judgement about all things but he himself is not subject to any man's judgement"

We Christians are spiritual people. The way we view situations is different from the way people of this world view it. Many at times, behind any physical occurrence, which the people of the world call *"ordinary"* we who are sensitive in the spiritual matters know that there are spiritual undertones.

For example, let me point out certain occurrences affecting the world now: homosexualism and lesbianism.

Homosexualism is man-to-man committing sexual immoralities while lesbianism is woman-to-woman committing the same act. People of the world explain it away that these people are free to do what they will; hence many countries have legalised its practise. But we know from spiritual perspective that this is the devil in operation, that there are evil spirits behind these acts. Homosexuals and lesbians are seriously under the bondage of *"the devil, who has taken them captive to do his wills."* (2 TIMOTHY 2: 26). We can put a stop to this evil act, firstly by taking the spiritual authority *"against principalities, against powers, against the rulers of the darkness of this world, against spiritual wickedness in high places."* (**EPHESIANS 6: 12**). When we defeat them spiritually then we can easily preach to the victims and they will repent and turn away from their sins.

Another good example is the recent murderous act among the youths in England. Youngsters between ages twelve and twenty-five killing one another with knives whilst the Government tries to curb this acts, it still continues. We know that ordinary physical effort cannot provide a permanent solution to this because in the realm of the spirit, demons are the ones influencing these youths. No one in his right mind will stab his fellow human being to death. Jesus Christ spoke about Satan that he is a murderer from the beginning (**JOHN 8: 44**). All evils in this present world is as a result of demonic influences .No wonder God called the Christians to war not against flesh and blood, that is, human beings, but against these evil spirits.

MAD MAN OF GADARA

Do you remember the situation in **MARK CHAPTER 5**? A mad man whom no one could tame; doctors had given up on him, the society had condemned him to his fate, he would scream in the tomb where he lived and cut himself with stone. If the medical doctors of our age were called to treat him, many tests would be carried out, many prescriptions would be made, medical names would be created for the cause of his madness yet there would be no cure for this man. This is because the origin of his problem is from the spiritual.

We Christians understand why some sicknesses defy medical solutions; it is because some evil spirits are at work in the life of the victim. Thank God for some Christian doctors who have the understanding of spiritual things, they easily discern the work of the devils over their patients and rebuke the evil spirits before they treat the patient medically. Satan is afraid of such doctors.

The life history of this mad man of Gadara changed dramatically when the Lord Jesus Christ, the spiritual man, stepped out of the boat to meet him.

MARK 5: 1-10

"They went across the lake to the region of the Gerasenes. When Jesus got out of the boat, a man with an evil spirit came out of the tomb to meet him. This man lived in the tombs, and no one could bind him anymore, not even with a chain. For he had often been chained hand and foot, but he tore the chains apart and broke the irons on his feet. No one was strong enough to subdue him. Night and day among the tombs and in the hills he would cry out and cut himself with stones. When he saw Jesus from a distance, he ran and fell on his knees in front of him. He shouted at the top of his voice, "what do you want with me, Jesus, Son of the Most High God? Swear to God that you won't torture me!" For Jesus had said to him, "Come out of this man, you evil spirit!" Then Jesus asked him, "What is your name?" "My name is Legion," he replied, "for we are many." And he begged Jesus again and again not to send them out of the area."

There is no medical apparatus that can detect this *"Legion"* of demons that had entered into this man to make him mad. It takes the Holy Spirit through the spiritually sensitive people to discern this kind of situation. This is exactly what the Lord Jesus Christ did; He discerned cast out those evil spirits.

You can notice something in VERSE 10 above that the demons *"begged Jesus again and again not to send them out of the area."* They are examples of territorial demons, which we have been talking about. Don't forget that Satan is a 'good' administrator.

Another important thing worth noticing in this scripture is in VERSE 15:

MARK 5: 15
"When they came to Jesus, they saw the man who had been possessed by the Legion of demons, sitting there, dressed and IN HIS RIGHT MIND; and they were afraid."

The man sat down with Jesus, well dressed and *"in his right mind"*. This is to say that in all these years, he was not in his right mind. This is exactly what we're saying. Many people who do evil and foolish things are not in their right minds otherwise they would hate to do it. In a similar manner Apostle Paul pointed out that the people who reject the gospel of Jesus Christ are not in their right mind because Satan and his demons veiled their minds.

2 Corinthians 4: 3, 4
"And even if our gospel is veiled, it is veiled to those who are perishing. The god of this age has blinded the minds of unbelievers, so that they cannot see the light of the gospel of the glory of Christ, who is the image of God."

This is why God has commissioned the Christians to battle against all dominion of the devils over the soul of men in this world so that they may be saved. The unfortunate thing is that many Christians also allow themselves to be veiled in their minds. They refuse to pray for spiritual understanding and to seek God's Word for revelation. For this purpose is this book written that it might be an eye opener. May God help us to rise up to our divine task.

CHAPTER TWELVE
DON'T ALLOW SATAN AND HIS AGENTS OPPRESS YOU |

In my early Christian life, I saw (and still see) many areas where Satan embarrasses the children of God. Although he has right to dominate those who reject the gospel, but surely, in the sight of God he has no spiritual right to touch any child of God who knows his or her standing before God in Christ. I often use the following illustration whenever I am addressing the children of God about their position before the devil: *"It is no news when you see a cat chasing a rat, but when a rat pursues a cat, surely there is a problem"*. In a similar way, when a child of God defeats the devil that is spiritually normal, but when the devil defeats or oppress any child of God it is really, really abnormal.

I have seen many of such abnormalities in Christendom: Satan afflicting Christians with sicknesses and diseases, blocking their path of progress, afflicting them with poverty, tormenting them in dreams, summoning their *'spirit-man'* for evil activities, killing their loved ones. Occultic people are oppressing Christians with charms and other occultic powers, demons inhabiting the body of Christians, demons having sexual intercourse with Christians and a lot more of these abnormalities.

Many Christians are afraid of the devil more than our glorious God. But, why? What has given the devil this audacity to molest the heirs of salvation? The Word of God provides the only answer, *"my people are destroyed for lack of knowledge"* (HOSEA 4:6). I, myself, have suffered greatly from the hand of the devil in my early christian-life; this had led me to study God's Word more and more for the truth to deal with this issue.

Thank God for His word, I can boldly declare it to the heavenlies and the whole world that Satan cannot stand before me anymore because God has opened my eyes to my position and authority in Christ. I know that Christ Jesus conquered the devil; I know also that I am in Christ, and that Christ Himself has given me the authority over all the works of the devil. God has also graciously shed light unto me to understand the activities of the spirit realm. I praise His holy name.

LUKE 10: 19
"I have given you authority to trample on the snakes and scorpions and to overcome all the power of the enemy; nothing will harm you."

THE TRUTH CONQUERS LIE

The best way to defeat lies is to really be acquainted with the truth. When you are well familiar with the original, you will easily detect any fake that may come your way. Satan is a fake! The father of all lies. The Lord Jesus tells us that he has no truth in him and cannot stand the truth. In order words, the only thing that conquers the devil is the truth of God's Word.

When you get the revelation understanding of God's Word, you will not but be bold to confront the devil, and surely, he will flee from you. The Bible says, *"Submit yourselves, then, to God. Resist the devil, and he will from you"* (JAMES 4:7). You cannot resist him with your own natural strength or wisdom. You can only do so by knowing the established Word of God, and then you too must first submit to the Word.

Watch out for anything contrary to the Word of God in your life and stand against it using the very Word of God. This is called the spiritual battle – the battle to enforce the truth over every lies. The Word of God will always prevail in every situation.

ACTS 19: 20 KJV
"So mightily grew the word of God and prevailed"

I remember one day, I prayed to God. I said,

"Lord my Father, show me from your Word all the truth I need to know to silence the devil completely over my life." I would frequently give myself to studying the Word of God with an expectant heart. Thanks to God many truths were revealed to me and I have been putting Satan to flight since then. Halleluah! Some of the revelations, which were revealed to me by the Holy Spirit, are what I am sharing with you in this book. You too can pray the prayer and give yourself diligently to the study of God's Word. The Holy Spirit will reveal many things to you. Don't forget that it is only the revelation of God's Word that defeats the devil.

Now I want to show you how you can live victoriously in your liberty purchased for you by the Lord Jesus Christ, and to overcome every manipulations of the devil against your existence.

This we'll do by prayers. Before we begin to pray let me remind you of the few things once again in order to prepare you for the prayers.

UNDERSTAND YOUR POSITION IN CHRIST

We have dealt with this in the earlier chapter, but as a reminder, let me point out who God says you are as you become born-again.

ONE

God in His sovereign power adopted you as His child, made you a joint-heir with Christ His Son. He breaks the authority of Satan over your life and translates you into the kingdom of His dear Son. He reconciles you unto Himself not counting your sins against you so that you become His treasured possession forever. He becomes your Eternal Father.

Apostle John summarises it in this way:

1 JOHN 3:1
"How great is the love the Father has lavished on us, that we should be called children of God! And that is what we are!"

Therefore let no one negotiate your sonship with you. You must always thank God for adopting you as His precious child. You must always confess in the place of prayer that you believe you are a child of God, and always claim the truth of the scripture showing this to you. You must always tell the devil in the place of prayer that you know you are in Christ as a child of God, and that he (Satan) has no authority over your life and anything that has to do with you.

TWO

You must know that not only are you a child of God but you are raised with Christ Jesus and seated with Him on the throne in heaven far above every authority of the devil. In other words you are not under Satan or his agents but spiritually you are above them all. Do not agree with anyone who makes you believe that Satan and his agents are stronger than you. Believe what God's Word says; confess it times without number unto yourself and loudly for the devils to hear in the place of prayer.

In my own case, for example, I will *normally say loud and clear in the place of prayer: "Let all the heavens hear this, let all principalities and power, and wicked spirits in the heavenly realm hear this, let the rulers of the darkness of this world hear this, let all the creatures of God hear this, that I am a son of God, joint heir with Christ, and I am seated with Christ in the heavenly realm; I am above all authority of the devil, God has given me authority in Christ Jesus to trample down and overcome all powers of the enemy nothing shall by any means hurt me...devil! Hear me, I am your boss, you are under me..."*

With childlike faith I confess these truths times without number. Each time I do this faith spring to life in me and satanic activities against my life becomes paralysed. I found out that God's Word is absolutely true and settled in heaven forever.

UNDERSTAND THE OPERATIONS OF SATAN AND HIS AGENTS

Do not forget what we treated in Chapter 5 of this book on the topic *"This Complicated World"*, devil and his agents are actively present in our world and doing evil continuously. He has two classes of agents working for him; first, he has the spirit agents – the fallen angels and demons, which Apostle Paul tells us about in **EPHESIANS 6:12**. These agents carry out the operations of Satan in this world like God's angels carry out God's instructions.

Apart from the spirit agents, devil also has human agents working for him in this world. These agents are everywhere. The human agents learn the ways of the devil and propagate his evil *"gospel"* in a similar way in which we as God's agents learn the ways of God and propagate his gospel. Demons and human agents of the devil cooperate to do the works of Satan in the same way that Christians cooperate with the Holy Spirit and angels of God to do the work of God.

Witches, wizards, occultic and idol priests, occult grand masters, people with familiar spirits and marine spirits, people who talk with the dead, those who evoke demons, and many more are human agents of the devil, they are everywhere carrying out the evil works of the devil.

Many a times we Christians do not know who is against us, we don't know who is jealous of our progress, or who we have offended and not ready to forgive us. Such people may be demonic or might consult the devil's agents to fight us spiritually. We must be prepared for them. In Chapter 4 we discussed the *"Movements in The Spirit Realm."*

Study it prayerfully and get ready to block all the attacks of the evil ones against your life. Fear not for God is with you!

Understand The Principles of The Spiritual Realm

If the devil and his agents will not oppress you, it is very compulsory that you take to heart the principles of the spiritual realm as we have dealt with it in Chapter 4 and other portions of this book. Don't forget the evil spiritual kingdom of the devil; do not forget his evil administration over this world, take to heart the territorial princes of the devil over families, communities cities, countries and nations.

Seek to fully understand the principle of movements in the spiritual realm: angels and demons move about in the spiritual realm, human spirits also move in the spiritual realm. Remember the principle of utterances; utterances are the messages carried by angels and demons in the spiritual realm, when there is no utterance then there will not be movement in realm of the spirit. Put all these to heart and use it against the devil and his agents in the place of prayer whenever they come against you. Ignorance is very dangerous in this case.

Take to heart that the Lord Jesus has prevailed in the spiritual realm, and at the mention of His Name all knee must bow. As you use the Name of Jesus against all the works of the devil, the Lord Himself shall manifest to destroy the works of the devil in your life, home, career and ministry.

One day while ministering in one of our church branches, I said to the people, *"Have you ever sat down to think on how somebody would chant incantation in Nigeria for example, calling upon the name of somebody for evil in Europe, and that person in Europe would experience that evil pronounced against him from Nigeria?"* The question is, what has transported the evil pronouncement from Nigeria to Europe? The simple answer is that a demon travels in the spiritual realm to deliver the message or the spirit-man of the victim is summoned from Europe to Nigeria.

As for me I always say boldly that there is no one who can project any demon against me because no demon can stand up against me, and no occultic power can summon my spirit-man for any evil manipulations in Jesus name.

Therefore as we understand our position in Christ over the devil, as we understand the operations of the devil and his cohorts, and the movements in the spiritual realm, we should then rise up to pray against every manipulations of the devil against our lives. God Himself will surely give us victory.

UNDERSTAND YOUR FOUNDATIONS BEFORE YOU CAME TO CHRIST

None of us fell down from heaven to come to this world; we were all born into different families. The family you were born into becomes your first foundation. You are automatically brought under the satanic powers ruling over that family. Every curses and evil covenants enslaving that family lineage also rules over you. This is one of the greatest spiritual principles and it is worth given keen attention to.

Let me show you a simple illustration from the scriptures: Abraham in the book of **GENESIS** went to a priest called Melchizedek and paid tithe to him. He did this while he was yet without any child (**GENESIS 14**). After some years Abraham gave birth to Isaac; Isaac gave birth to Jacob and Jacob gave birth twelve sons, which became the nation of Israel today. Don't forget that Jacob also bears Israel, so the nation of Israel is also called the nation of Jacob. The point here is that a single man Abraham became the father or the ancestor of the nation of Israel.

The book of **HEBREWS** in the New Testaments sheds a great light of understanding to us about the case:

HEBREWS 7: 9,10
"One might even say that Levi, who collects the tenth, paid the tenth through Abraham, because when Melchizedek met Abraham, Levi was still in the body of his ancestor."

God counted it that Levi, fourth generation to Abraham paid the tithe to priest Melchizedek through Abraham even while he had not yet been born. Levi in the loins of Abraham paid the tithe together with his ancestor.

This is to show you that everything that your ancestors in the family where you are born into did affects your life because you are a descendant of that family. In the case of Abraham he paid the tithe to the priest of the Most High God because he worshiped God, so his God becomes the God of his descendants up till now. God will normally refer to Himself as the God of Abraham, Isaac and Jacob in the Bible, He would normally tell the Israelites that "I am the God of your fore fathers." He is their God because He is the God of their ancestors. Let this be clear to us that God or gods of your ancestors lawfully in the spiritual realm becomes your God or gods until you rise up to renounce the God or gods.

Let me ask you this heart searching question, what god did your ancestors serve? Our fore fathers in Africa had served the devil himself through so many idols, and those demon gods behind the idols claims authority over all the descendants of such families.

You as a person may not be aware of any idol in your immediate family but if you ask questions and trace your ancestral generation backward you will clearly find out that you are under the control of such evil gods. Those gods will directly or indirectly demand worship from those under their control.

Any god that is served would have covenant with his worshippers. Violation of such covenants would invite curses and punishment from the god. You, as a descendant of the family you are born into, have ancestral covenants with the gods of your fathers.

Evil Foundations Built By Your Errors

Apart from your ancestral foundations, your own errors could create another foundation in your life to give Satan and his agents rights to oppress you. Your sins, your involvement in any occultism, swearing a oath before any evil priest, eating food sacrificed to idols, making blood covenant with somebody, sexual immoralities, abortions and so on. All these evil foundations create openings in your life for Satan and his agents to attack you. These openings must be closed to prevent satanic attacks.

Now That You Are In Christ

Now that you have become a born again Christian, you have created another foundation for yourself in Christ; you have entered into a covenant to serve the living God of heaven and the earth by the blood of Jesus Christ. In Christ Jesus you have a new ancestor because God has totally changed your ancestors. Please meditate on the topic we treated in Chapter 10 of this book, *"The Family Members Of God's Kingdom."* But be sure that evil gods and covenants of your earthly ancestors will fight against you. And those covenants will always create openings in your life in the realm of the spirit for satanic manipulations if you do not do anything to break them.

In order for you to be free from such satanic embarrassments as I always call it, you must rise up and renounce the gods and break their evil covenants and curses by the blood of Jesus. The blood of Jesus is the greatest blood covenant that destroys every other blood covenants, no controversy about that. You must confess to the devil that you know that you now belong to God's family. Satan cannot withstand the truth of God's Word; he must bow to it.

If you know of any foundations you have created by your own errors you must also renounce them all. We may not know all the evil foundations, which have opened us up in the spiritual realm, but through prayers Holy Spirit will reveal them to us so that we might pray seriously to secure our total deliverance. This is an active spiritual warfare; the neglect of this truth is very dangerous.

CHAPTER 13

PRAYERS AND CONFESSIONS

PRAYERS FOR SPIRITUAL ILLUMINATIONS

These prayers you are about to pray will open your spiritual illuminations to every works of the devil around you; it will open up your dream life for divine revelation. Covered works of the devil will be uncovered before you, and if you have not been dreaming at all or have been having polluted dreams or dreaming and forgetting, these prayers will help you in Jesus name.

SCRIPTURES FOR MEDITATIONS

GENESIS 1: 3,4; HEBREWS 4: 13; MATTHEW 10: 26; PSALM 139: 12; ISAIAH 60: 1-3; DANIEL 2: 20-22; JOHN 8: 12.

Meditate thoroughly on the above scriptures and digest them before you take these prayer points. Make plans for at least 3 days for the prayers and add fasting. When praying quote the scriptures at will, as directed by the Holy Spirit in your heart. God is on your side.

PRAYER POINTS

1. Oh Lord my God henceforth I refuse to dwell in spiritual blackout in Jesus name.
2. My Father, command your light to shine all around my spiritual situations.
3. Oh Lord my God, every secret works of the devil against my life, let it be uncovered by fire in Jesus name.
4. My heavenly Father, naked the devil before me now in Jesus name.
5. Every satanic power that keeps my dream life in darkness let them be disgraced by the brightness of God's light.
6. My heavenly Father, everything that has opened my life up for satanic invaders, reveal them and show me the way out.
7. Holy Ghost fire consume every stronghold of the devil against my dream life.
8. Whatever you are showing me Lord, help me to see it well.
9. Lord take away pollution from my spiritual sight.
10. Purge me completely with your fire oh Lord so that I may see clearly.
11. You satanic powers that corrupt my spiritual

visions and dreams, be consumed by the Holy Ghost fire.

12. No demon shall gain entrance into my life to show me anything in Jesus name.

13. Every secret works of the devil against my life, my home, my business, my ministry etc Holy Spirit reveal them to me from time to time.

14. I cleanse my dream life with the blood of Jesus.

15. Henceforth by the power of God, I walk in the divine light in my dream life.

16. Henceforth my dream life becomes a spiritual television controlled by the Holy Spirit.

17. Lord you are the source of revelation in my life, to you only is my life opened and not to the devil or his agents.

Deliverance From Evil Ancestral Bondages (7 Days Fasting & Prayer)
Scriptures For Meditations
Ezekiel 18:1-4; Colossians 1:12-14; Obadiah 1: 17; 1john.3: 8; 1 Corinthians 11:23-25.

Prayer Points

1. Spend quality time in the presence of God with praise, worship and thanksgiving. Singing melody in your heart with psalms, hymns and choruses.

2. Confess your sins and plead the blood of Jesus Christ. Ask for the grace to overcome sins.

3. Seek His face for the purification of your spirit, soul and body.

4. S oak yourself into the blood of Jesus Christ and the fire of the Holy Ghost.

Now! Take The Following Prayer Points Seriously:

5. Every covenant that bound my life to the kingdom of darkness, the blood of Jesus destroys it now.

6. Every covenant that bound my life to the evil authority ruling the earthly family where I was born, the blood of Jesus destroy it now.

7. Every covenant that bound my life to the demonic Idols worshiped in my earthly ancestral family, I

break the covenant now by the blood of Jesus. (MENTION THE NAME OF THE IDOL IF YOU KNOW ANY, IF YOU DON'T KNOW JUST PRAY IN FAITH)

8. Every evil covenant which I was taken into from the womb or when I was very young, I separate myself from it now and I break the covenant by the blood of Jesus.

9. Every covenant that bound my life to the kingdom of darkness through incision, food eaten, bathing, soap used, clothe used etc, I destroy it by the blood of Jesus.

10. Evil hereditary characters that manifests in my life through my parents (father or mother); I destroy it in the name of Jesus.

11. Evil ancestral blood that flows in my body, Doctor Jesus draw it out now.

12. From now henceforth my blood has become the blood of Jesus Christ.

13. Evil authority that controls my life and destiny through my parents, your authority is rendered useless in my life and destiny in Jesus name.

14. Hence forth I come out (spiritually) from the family where I was born and I enter into the family of God in Christ Jesus.

15. You evil monitoring spirit assigned to monitor my destiny, you have no right to afflict me, I rebuke you, get out of my life in Jesus name.

16. You spirit of poverty, retrogression, hardship, blockage, bareness, aborted breakthrough etc, leave my life in Jesus name.

17. Evil utterances spoken from any demonic source, assigned to work against the will of God in my life, such utterances are silenced forever in Jesus name.

18. Every finished work of the devil against my life, is brought to nothing forever in Jesus name.

19. Oh Lord my God show your power over the kingdom of darkness for my sake.

20. Oh my God! Uncover every manipulations of the devil before me in Jesus name.

21. You strong man in my earthly family lineage that has been causing problem in my life and my marriage, the Lord consume you with fire before me in Jesus name.

22. Every blockage at the edge of success be buried in the lake of fire in Jesus name.

23. Today is the day that the Lord has made, today marks the separation of my destiny (spiritually) from my earthly mother and father's lineage in Jesus name.

24. I have been translated from the kingdom of darkness to the kingdom of His Dear son – the Kingdom of God and His Light in Jesus name.

NOTE: ANY DREAM OR REVELATION MUST BE NOTED. DO NOT HESITATE TO CALL FOR COUNSELLING IF NECESSARY.

Confession of Faith for Liberty and Breakthroughs

The confession of faith below is a mighty weapon of utterance to silence every accusing mouth of the enemy. As you confess them into the heavenlies times without number, God backs you up and take to effect everything you say according to His Word.

I have written these few out for you as examples. You too can get more for yourself as you study and meditate on the Word of God.

Confessions

- God has saved me and translated me into the kingdom of Christ – His dear Son. I am no longer in the kingdom of Satan because Christ has set me free. No demon or any satanic agent can rule over my life; I am now in the kingdom of God.

- I died with Christ, was buried with him and rose up with him unto new life. Old things about my life that the devil knew about has passed away and everything about my life is new in Christ Jesus. I am carrying the life of Christ; He is my life.

- I am seated with Christ on the throne in the highest heaven far above every authority of the devil. He has given me the authority to trample upon snakes and scorpions and to overcome every power of the devil; nothing shall by any means hurt me.

- The Spirit of the Lord dwells in my heart therefore I walk about in liberty, I sleep and dream in liberty, and my home is in liberty. My business and ministry are in liberty etc. No forces of the enemy shall subject me to bondage.

- No weapon fashioned against me shall prosper. By the authority of the Lord I condemn every evil tongue that rise up against me.

- I overcome and subdue every territorial demon in this area where I live, in this area where I work (mention the areas) etc.

- The fire of the Lord goes before me and clears my way to the top. Every demonic roadblock against me is consumed by Holy Ghost fire. No satanic territorial prince can hold my blessings down, and I am matching up to my glorious destiny; the gates of hell shall not stop me.

- In the land of the living I am manifesting the glory of Christ from time to time. Everyone sees the glory of God all around me. Favour surrounds me as a shield; every creature favours me compulsorily by the power of the Lord who pronounced me favoured.

Amen!

Your testimony is certain. God be with you.